Brett Favre

FOOTBALL  SUPERSTARS

FOOTBALL ⬤ SUPERSTARS

Brett Favre

Rachel A. Koestler-Grack

CHELSEA HOUSE
PUBLISHERS
An imprint of Infobase Publishing

BRETT FAVRE

Chelsea House
An imprint of Infobase Publishing
132 West 31st Street
New York NY 10001

Library of Congress Cataloging-in-Publication Data
Koestler-Grack, Rachel A., 1973-
  Brett Favre / Rachel A. Koestler-Grack.
      p. cm. — (Football superstars)
  Includes bibliographical references and index.
  ISBN 978-0-7910-9690-1 (hardcover)
  1. Favre, Brett—Juvenile literature. 2. Football players—United States—Biography—Juvenile literature. 3. Quarterbacks (Football)—United States—Biography—Juvenile literature. I. Title. II. Series.

  GV939.F29K64 2008
  796.332092—dc22   2007040949

Chelsea House books are available at special discounts when purchased in bulk quantities for businesses, associations, institutions, or sales promotions. Please call our Special Sales Department in New York at (212) 967-8800 or (800) 322-8755.

You can find Chelsea House on the World Wide Web at http://www.chelseahouse.com

Text design and composition by Erik Lindstrom
Cover design by Ben Peterson
Cover printed by Yurchak Printing, Landisville, Pa.
Book printed and bound by Yurchak Printing, Landisville, Pa.
Printed in the United States of America

This book is printed on acid-free paper.

All links and Web addresses were checked and verified to be correct at the time of publication. Because of the dynamic nature of the Web, some addresses and links may have changed since publication and may no longer be valid.

CONTENTS

Tough Guy

Brett Favre did not have the slightest idea about what to expect as he trotted onto the field to play **quarterback** for the Green Bay Packers at the Oakland Coliseum on the night of Monday, December 22, 2003. Part of him wanted to play better than he had ever played during his **National Football League (NFL)** career. But he had never thrown a football under circumstances such as these before. In the years leading up to this game against the Oakland Raiders, Favre had always told himself that he could handle almost any situation, on or off the field. He had never prepared himself for what happened the day before the game, though. His dad—"Big Irv"—had died. He would be playing against the Raiders in a Monday Night Football game in front of a national television audience. Everyone watching would know what had happened, what he was going through.

THE CALL

The day before the game, Favre had joined some of his team-mates for a round of golf. While they were on the course, fellow quarterback Doug Pederson's cell phone rang. Favre's wife, Deanna, was on the other end. After talking to her for a moment, Pederson's expression changed. Favre could tell it was not good news. Pederson pulled the phone down from his ear and broke the news to Favre—Favre's father had died of a heart attack. He handed the phone to Favre, who stood stunned for what seemed forever before he could talk to Deanna.

Favre had always been close to his father. As a child, he would roam the **sidelines** while his father coached high school football. Irvin Favre, or Irv, as he was more commonly known, attended every one of Brett's games since Pee Wee football in the fifth grade. In high school, Big Irv was Brett's coach—the one who taught him to truly love the game. The tragic news hit Favre hard. His first thoughts were of his family—his mom and brothers and sister—back in Mississippi. But Favre had another family to consider as well—his football family. His teammates and coaches depended on him, and he depended on them. The Packers needed to win against Oakland to keep their playoff hopes alive. Could they do it without him?

After he got off the phone with Deanna, Favre met with Packers head coach Mike Sherman. Right away, Sherman promised to support Favre no matter what decision he made—play or head home. Favre told him that he planned to play against the Raiders, and he wanted to talk to the rest of the players at that night's team meeting. He also said he wanted Deanna with him in California as soon as possible. Immediately, Sherman booked a flight for her from Green Bay to Oakland.

Favre knew his decision to play on Monday night would bring mixed reactions. Some fans would say, "I hope he plays great." Others would say, "He should have gone home to be with his family." However, Favre did what his dad would have wanted. Irv would have wanted Brett to play, not just for himself but for his teammates. As a coach, Irv knew how much work the coaches and players put into each game. He would not have wanted Brett to let them down when there was so much at stake.

Almost everyone on the Packers knew Irv. At the team meeting that night, Favre said, "I'm with you, and if you ever wondered before, you don't have to wonder now." He assured them that he would be there for his "Packers family" on Monday night. By the time he was done speaking, there was not a dry eye in the room.

The sun rose and fell on Monday, the same way it always had. It was time for Favre to face the Raiders. He would have to clear his head and focus on the task at hand. As any NFL fan knows, it is never easy to win a game on the road, no matter what kind of record the opponent has. In Oakland, Raiders fans, collectively known as Raider Nation, are notorious for being some of the toughest, meanest, and rowdiest supporters in the league. The fans behind the north **end zone**—the Black Hole—dress up in wild costumes that make them look like a nasty biker gang. As Favre stepped out onto the field, he was not sure if he was ready to face the rough crowd. Much to his surprise, the Raiders' fans gave him a standing ovation. Obviously, they knew what had happened. It was the first time members of the Black Hole ever applauded a visiting player.

On this night, Favre was not his usually confident self. His mouth was so dry he could hardly swallow, and he was having trouble breathing. He paused for a moment to wipe the sweat off his forehead. When he looked down to adjust his wristbands, he noticed his hands were shaking like two leaves in a breeze. Favre took a deep breath, tugged on his facemask,

Green Bay quarterback Brett Favre enters the huddle during the Packers' Monday Night Football game with the Oakland Raiders on December 22, 2003. Favre's father, Irvin, had died of a heart attack the day before, but Brett felt that his father would have wanted him to play in the game.

and tried to settle down. He doubted he could even complete a 10-**yard** pass.

Favre felt a ton of pressure to perform well. Much was riding on the game, and he did not want to let his fans down. Of course, if he played lousy, he would have an excuse. But Favre did not want to make excuses, even if his father's death had an effect on him. The voice of his dad echoed in his head. In his book *Favre*, Brett recounted what Irv would have said: "Son, once you decide to play, you go out there and play your ass off." That was exactly what Favre wanted to do.

THE GAME OF HIS LIFE

As he leaned into the offensive **huddle**, Favre said, "Hey, we need this game. Here we go." The first play was a **handoff** to **tailback** Ahman Green, who gained 10 yards. So far, so good, Favre thought. After a two-yard loss, a penalty, and a six-yard run by Green, the Packers faced third-and-11. Favre lined up in the **shotgun formation**. After the **center** snapped the ball to him, Favre's first read was **wide receiver** Donald Driver, who was coming across the middle of the field. Favre waited for Driver to clear Oakland **cornerback** Charles Woodson, but just as he was about to throw the pass, he caught a glimpse of a Raiders **safety** coming down to cover the play. Making a quick decision, Favre checked down to his second option— wide receiver Robert Ferguson on a 10-yard comeback. Favre assumed Ferguson would be right where he was supposed to be, so he turned to throw. Noticing that Ferguson was not there, Favre adjusted. Apparently, Ferguson had gotten a step ahead of the cornerback and had just continued running up the sideline. Fortunately, Ferguson spotted the ball and made an amazing catch for a 24-yard gain. Upon seeing the spectacular play, Favre realized that the game might just turn out OK after all.

A few plays later, Favre called a corner route to **tight end** Wesley Walls. After the **snap**, Favre rolled to his left. To most fans watching the game, it looked as if a Raiders **linebacker** had Walls well covered. But Favre knew exactly where to throw the ball. If he put the ball where only Walls could catch it—while the linebacker was peeking back to look in the **pocket**—the play could work. One of Favre's strengths (and weaknesses) is that he feels he can complete any pass. This time was no different. Walls made the catch in the back of the end zone—**touchdown**!

After that first touchdown, Favre felt a whole lot better about the Packers' chances of winning. However, he had no

Brett Favre and his wife, Deanna, walk off the field after the Packers' 41-7 win over the Oakland Raiders. Despite playing with a heavy heart, Favre had one of the best games of his career, completing 22 of 30 passes for 399 yards and four touchdowns.

idea that he would throw three more first-half touchdowns in taking the Packers to a 31-7 halftime lead. In the first half, the Packers had six possessions. They played out: touchdown, touchdown, **field goal**, touchdown, **punt**, and touchdown. The second touchdown pass was a 23-yarder to wide receiver Javon Walker. In Favre's opinion, it may have been his second- or third-best throw of the season. After that play, Favre thought something special might be going on.

For Favre, it was the greatest half of football he had played in his career. He completed 15 of 18 passes for 311 yards and four touchdowns. And he did it all under the most difficult of circumstances. The second half was just as satisfying. By the end of the game, the Pack—as their fans call them—racked up 548 yards, the third-most in franchise history. The Packers held the Raiders scoreless in the second half to reel in a 41-7 win.

Some people wondered if divine power helped the Packers win that night. Favre could not really say, although it was the kind of game his dad would have loved. In an amazing show of camaraderie, Favre's teammates rallied around him. He may have made some of the best throws of the season, but his compatriots made some difficult plays look easy. At the end of the game, Favre had completed 22 of 30 passes for 399 yards. His **passer rating** of 154.9 rocketed off the charts.

The Monday night game against the Oakland Raiders was a vivid illustration of Brett Favre's character. Once again, he proved his ability to soar above adversity and embrace challenges. In fact, he had one of the best years of his professional career, in what would turn out to be a difficult stretch in his personal life. No wonder *Men's Journal* named him the

MOST PASSES COMPLETED IN NFL HISTORY

NUMBER	PLAYER
5,377	Brett Favre, Atlanta, 1991; Green Bay, 1992–2006
4,967	Dan Marino, Miami, 1983–1999
4,123	John Elway, Denver, 1983–1998

"Toughest Guy in America" in its March 2004 issue. Through the 2007 season, Favre had started an incredible 253 consecutive games during his 17-year NFL career. Actually, Favre started his impressive streak of perfect attendance earlier than most athletes. During his childhood, he went 10 years without missing a single day of school. Today, he holds several NFL records and ranks in the top five in virtually every other statistical category for NFL quarterbacks. He is the only player

PLAYING WITH THE HURT

The March 2004 issue of *Men's Journal* named Brett Favre "The Toughest Guy in America." When Favre first heard the news, he thought it was a joke. As it turned out, however, it was a serious poll. A panel of 100 experts in various professions voted for their toughest guy, based on perseverance, fearlessness, pain threshold, and modesty. Favre was up against some tough competition. The runner-up was Michael Weisskopf, a senior correspondent for *Time* magazine, who spent time in Baghdad, covering the War in Iraq. While Weisskopf was riding in an open-air Humvee, a rebel insurgent tossed a grenade into Weisskopf's vehicle. He instinctively grabbed the grenade and threw it out as it exploded. He saved the life of everyone on board but lost his right hand. To Favre, Weisskopf was not just tough—he was a hero.

As Favre thumbed through the article, he winced each time he was reminded about an injury he was forced to play through during his career. In 1992, he had to overcome a first-degree separation of his left shoulder. He played with a deep thigh bruise in 1993 and a severely bruised hip in 1994. In 1995, he seriously sprained his left ankle and got the

in NFL history to be named Most Valuable Player (MVP) three times. During his NFL career, he has been selected to play in nine Pro Bowl games. He holds the NFL records for most career pass completions (5,377), most seasons with 20 or more touchdown passes (13), most seasons with 30 or more touchdown passes (5), and several others. Coming from a small town on the Mississippi Bayou, Brett Favre has proved that greatness can grow out of the tiniest seed.

wind knocked out of him twice. He sprained his right thumb against the Denver Broncos in 1999. At Tampa Bay in 2000, he sprained his left foot. He also suffered with tendonitis in his right elbow that year. In 2002, he sprained the lateral collateral ligament in his left knee. He played with a broken right thumb in 2003.

Favre admits that as he gets older the injuries seem to become more prevalent and take longer to heal. After many Sundays, he was not sure if he could start the next week. But somehow, it always seemed to work out. At the time of the *Men's Journal* article, Favre had pocketed 208 consecutive starts, including playoff games—an NFL record for quarterbacks.

Favre attributes most of his toughness to the way he was raised. When he was growing up, his dad—who was also his coach—told him never to lie on the field. He did not like to see any crybaby stuff, players rolling around as if they had suffered a severe injury. From an early age, Favre learned to play with the hurt. While he is not sure his laundry list of injuries makes him the toughest guy in America, he agrees that it definitely makes him one of the most beaten up.

On the Rotten Bayou

October 10, 1969, was a Friday—football night at St. John High School, in Gulfport, Mississippi, where Irv Favre was a coach. Earlier in the day, Irv's wife, Bonita, went into labor with her second child. Throughout the day, Irv needled her to hurry up, because he had a game to coach. Luckily, Brett Lorenzo Favre was polite enough to show up in time for his dad to make the game. He was a big boy at 9 pounds, 15 ounces—certainly big enough to play football, his father probably thought. In his autobiography, *Favre: For the Record*, Brett Favre recalled what the doctor told his mother shortly after he was delivered. The doctor joked, "He's a big one, Bonita. Right now he's back in the nursery doing push-ups." That night, St. John was scheduled to play the Hancock North Central Hawks. Little did the Favres know that their son would be starting his legendary career as a football player at Hancock 14 years later.

GROWING UP IN A SMALL TOWN

Brett grew up along the Rotten Bayou, just outside the small town of Kiln, in southern Mississippi, 12 miles (19 kilometers) north of the Gulf of Mexico. The Favres owned a two-bedroom house and 52 acres (21 hectares) of land, surrounded on three sides by water—so close the Favre boys could spit into it off their deck. Scott, three years Brett's senior, was the oldest of the Favre children. Next came Brett, then a few years later Jeff was born, and, finally, sister Brandi would round out the Favre clan. When the local fire department required every street to have a name, the Favres appropriately named theirs Irvin Favre Drive. However, the actual street sign was misspelled, so their address became 1213 Irvin Farve Drive. After all, no one else lived on the red-clay dirt road.

With a population of slightly more than 2,000, the small town of Kiln (pronounced "Kill") does not offer too much excitement. There are no movie theaters or shopping malls. Downtown consists of a yellow caution light, surrounded by a few businesses. According to Favre, the closest thing to a speed bump would be an occasional dead raccoon in the middle of the road. Favre described Kiln as the kind of place where people work on cars all day, party all night, and wrap it all up with a few barroom brawls.

But Brett liked the way the cozy town brought him close to family and friends. Grandpa French and Grandma French (whom Brett called Mee-Maw) lived in a trailer across a clearing from his house. In a tiny house next door lived his aunt Kay Kay. Plenty of Brett's aunts, uncles, and cousins also lived nearby. Brett's grandpa owned Bennie French's Tavern, a bar and restaurant on the beach in nearby Bay Saint Louis. According to Favre, his grandma served the best gumbo, shrimp creole, and red beans and rice on the Gulf Coast. Mee-Maw used to tell young Brett that Grandpa knew famed gangster Al Capone and claimed the notorious outlaws Bonnie and Clyde had stopped at the tavern on their way to Louisiana, where they were killed. Many days after school, Brett and his siblings would run around on the beach outside the bar or ride

FAVRE'S ON THE BAYOU

Food is certainly an important part of Favre family history. Perhaps it all started with Grandpa and Grandma French's restaurant—Bennie French's Tavern, where Grandma Mee-Maw served the best gumbo, shrimp creole, and red beans and rice on the Gulf Coast. In 1999, the Favre family decided to officially document their favorite recipes in the *Favre Family Cookbook: Three Generations of Cajun and Creole Cooking from the Gulf Coast*. Apparently, that was not enough for Brett's brothers, Scott and Jeff, though.

In 2001, they came to Bonita Favre with a business venture. Why not open a restaurant in southern Mississippi? They wanted Bonita and Irv to join them in this business venture. At first, Bonita told them absolutely not. Growing up, she had watched her parents put in long, hard hours at their restaurant. She did not want to spend her life that way. After some further thought, though, she reconsidered. As long as the boys could provide good management and it was not a 24/7 job, she decided that she would invest in the restaurant. On May 1, 2001, they opened Favre's on the Bayou. Their motto was, "Casual dining at its best."

The restaurant was a huge hit. A couple of weeks after opening, the Favres welcomed their first Mother's Day crowd. Bonita had no idea just how busy it would be. When Grandma

around the tables and stools on their Big Wheels. Everybody in Kiln knew the Favre boys. Even today, when Favre goes home, townsfolk slap him on the back and reminisce about the days when little Brett would run between their legs. Eventually after Grandpa Bennie's death, Mee-Maw sold the tavern. But at least Brett was still able to enjoy her famous home-cooked dishes.

Mee-Maw came in for a bite, Bonita told her to hurry up and eat because she needed the table. The day before, Bonita had asked her friend Pat to drop by around three in the afternoon. She figured by that time the crowd would have thinned out a bit. The moment Pat walked in the door, Bonita put her to work in the kitchen wrapping silverware in napkins.

Before he died, Irv was the restaurant's ambassador. He loved meeting and greeting guests. He had his own corner stool at the bar from which he would watch Packers games on television or shoot the breeze with patrons. The Favres especially welcomed the droves of Packers fans who visited the restaurant. Guests from throughout the state of Wisconsin dropped in for a Favre-cooked meal. The Packers fans were thrilled to meet Brett's parents and the rest of the Favre clan. In Brett and Bonita's book, *Favre*, Bonita extends her down-home hospitality. "If you come to Southern Mississippi," she said, "please mark Favre's on the Bayou one of your destinations." Sadly, the restaurant was destroyed by Hurricane Katrina, which devastated the Gulf Coast region of Alabama, Louisiana, and Mississippi in August 2005. Today, all that remains of the restaurant is a cement slab and the sign. The family has not yet decided whether or not they will rebuild it.

Almost every Saturday, Brett camped out in front of the television watching *Tarzan*. Each episode, Tarzan wrestled alligators, man-eating snakes, or some other terrifying creature. Many kids probably thought the jungle was worlds away. For Brett, however, Tarzan's world was much like his own. He saw gators and snakes all the time. If he had wanted to, he could have jumped in the Rotten Bayou and wrestled just about anything Tarzan did. The alligators were so common around Brett's house that they actually ate four of the family dogs. These dogs were not small pooches, either. There was a collie named Fluffy, a Saint Bernard named Whiskey, Bullet the German shepherd, and a chocolate Lab they called Lucky.

However, the missing dogs did not seem to scare the boys. They swam in the water anyway and spent time playing on the wharf. When they were young, though, they could not go down to the bayou without an adult. Scott and Brett even tried to make pets of the alligators once. One day after school, the two boys were home alone. Brett was about 8 years old at the time, Scott around 11. They stood near the river's edge throwing rocks at a pine tree on the other side. Then, they spotted three alligators swimming around in the water. Brett thought it would be fun to feed them, so he ran into the house and grabbed some cookies. The alligators gobbled them up. During the next few days, the boys quickly found out just how much alligators like cookies. Each day, the same three gators would be waiting there when the boys got home from school. They tossed out as many cookies as they could find in the cupboards. At first, they thought it was cool—until Irv got home early from football practice one day. Irv was pretty strict about messing with alligators. By the time Irv pulled into the yard, the three gators had grown tired of waiting for their cookies and were making their way from the river to the house. Irv ran to the house, snatched his shotgun, and fired several shots over the gators' heads. The alligators quickly slid back into the river. That was the last time Brett and his brother fed the alligators.

FOOTBALL DESTINY

A mutual friend introduced Irvin "Chief" Favre to 17-year-old Bonita French at a beach party in Henderson Point—her hometown. As it turned out, the two had much in common—they both liked sports. Irv played football and baseball, and Bonita was a basketball player. Irv was a good enough pitcher to play both college baseball and semiprofessional ball. From the beginning, sports were a big part of their relationship. However, Bonita almost blew her chance with Irv. When she came to visit him for homecoming, Irv asked if she noticed anything different about him. Earlier in the football season, he had broken his ankle and just had the cast removed. Puzzled, Bonita had to admit that she did not see anything different. Irv got so upset he threw his corsage at her. Luckily, though, he got over it.

One night, Irv drove Bonita to the baseball field at nearby Perkinston, Mississippi. There, he asked her to marry him. As it turned out, the proposal at a ball field was a fitting beginning for the couple. In the years ahead, the couple spent many days and nights at football and baseball fields throughout Mississippi.

In 1971, Irv took an assistant football coach job at Hancock North Central High School, and Kiln became their home for the next 25 years. Bonita dressed Scott and Brett in mascot outfits for every game. Brett's path to a life of football began as soon as he could toddle around the sidelines. Both parents were physical education teachers at Hancock North Central. Bonita was also a special education teacher, and in the summer, she worked as the lifeguard director in Diamondhead, Mississippi. In addition to phys ed, Irv taught driver's training. For a while, Bonita coached the girls' basketball team. However, she decided one Favre coach was enough when Scott fell in the bleachers and cut his head one night when she was coaching her team.

All the Favre boys were introduced to sports at a young age. Brett was three years old when he got his first football uniform—complete with a helmet and shoulder pads—for a Christmas present. Not long after, his parents bought him a baseball uniform. The boys played a brutal form of football in the yard almost every day. They hosed down the lawn, suited up in their football pads, and knocked heads in the mud. By the time they hobbled back to the house, at least one of them usually had a smashed nose, mangled finger, or some other injury. A good deal of arguing and pushing took place on that home field, but there were few fights. From time to time, the boys would storm away from each other in anger. But the next day, they would return to the field as if nothing had happened.

A game the boys liked to play was one they invented called "goal line." Scott and Brett played defense, and Jeff took the ball on offense. Play started five yards from the **goal line**. Jeff would have four plays to try to score. In this game, there was no running around the older boys. Jeff had to run through them. Many times, Jeff took quite a beating from his big brothers. Even as the boys got older, they still played goal line—even when Scott was in college.

From the time the boys were young, Bonita devoted her life to being a sports mom. She drove the kids to Little League games and Pee Wee football and spent many hours working the concession stands. Both parents offered their total support for the children's activities. They never missed a game Brett played in, from Little League through college football. In college, Brett played in 42 games, and his parents were there for every one of them. When he was a kid, he took their presence for granted. He thought that they should be at all of his games. But as he got older, he realized how lucky he was. Once, Brett asked his mom why she worked so hard to attend all of their games. She explained that her dad had missed her

Brett Favre's parents, Bonita and Irvin, encouraged their children to play sports when they were growing up. In fact, the family's lives revolved around football, because Irv was the head coach at the local high school, Hancock North Central. Bonita is pictured here in October 2005 at a signing in Hattiesburg, Mississippi, for her book *Favre*, which details Brett's life and football career.

high school graduation. She did not want any of the kids to feel that kind of hurt.

Although she was a tough woman who spoke her mind, Bonita often spoiled her kids. Of course, there were times she punished the boys and Brandi when they got out of line. Irv dealt out most of the punishment—and chores. When Bonita went shopping, the boys begged to join her. They knew what was in store for them if they stayed home. As soon as Bonita's car was out of sight, Irv would work their "tails off." He would grab a few rakes and toss them to the boys. "Let's get after it," he would say, as Brett recalled in *Favre: For the Record*. Every morning, Bonita was up by 6:00 A.M. to get breakfast for the family; and breakfast was always something hot—eggs, pancakes, or biscuits and gravy. When the boys were in high school, she would cook an extra-special breakfast buffet on Fridays. She called it "Touchdown Breakfast," because Friday was game night. Brett did not realize how spoiled he was until he got to college and was eating Pop-Tarts and cold cereal for breakfast.

When he was in fifth grade, Brett finally got to play in his first organized football game—a jamboree, which is four teams playing round-robin, or against every other team. That Saturday morning, Irv decided to stop and get a haircut on the way to the game. Irv would only go to one barber. Brett could never understand why his father was so particular. After all, Irv wore a flattop cut—not a challenging hairstyle. The barbershop was in Gulfport, Mississippi, a half hour away from Bay Saint Louis, where the jamboree was to be played. By the time Irv and Brett arrived, the game had already started. But the coach put Brett in right away at split end. On the first play, he caught a pass and got **tackled**. When he came down, he landed on the ball and got the wind knocked out of him. He was sprawled out on the ground, gasping for air, thinking he was going to die.

Finally, when he caught his breath, he burst into tears and staggered to the sidelines. "I hate playing split end," Brett told his coach. "I want to play quarterback." Perhaps feeling a little sorry for Brett, the coach put him in at quarterback for the second game of the jamboree. Brett ran for two touchdowns and threw for one more. It was quite a thrill for Brett. On the sidelines, the cheerleaders were jumping and cheering for him. Brett looked over at them, and in the true style of a fifth grader, he decided that quarterback was a cool **position** to play. From that day on, he wanted to be a quarterback.

However, there were some drawbacks to playing quarterback in grade school. For one thing, Brett's helmet was more like a lineman's than a quarterback's—there was a vertical bar across the front that Brett felt was restrictive. So in seventh grade, Brett finally took a hacksaw and cut the bar off. He wanted to look like a professional quarterback.

Early on, Irv could tell that Brett had a future at quarterback. He was not only talented but also big for his age, which helped. While he could play better than most, though, he was not an exceptional player. What made him stand out was his competitiveness. Even in Pee Wee football, Brett showed the aggression and smarts that all great players need. He was a mean kid when it came to playing sports. He hit hard and threw hard. And he played to win. He also knew that he excelled at throwing the football. In grade school, he often stopped by his dad's football practice after school. On the sidelines, he would launch the football just as far as the high school quarterback could throw it. By the time he entered high school, Brett was ready to take the next step. And with his dad as the head coach, there was no way around it, anyway.

Football Under Big Irv

During high school, many of Brett Favre's friends would come up to him and say, "Ah, man, I'd hate for my dad to be my coach." They saw firsthand just how hard his dad was on him. Sometimes Brett might have felt that way, too. But he admitted that the rules and strictness were good for him—and his game. Irv—or Big Irv as Brett liked to call him—wanted Brett to concentrate on football, lifting weights, and running.

On Friday nights after football games, many of his teammates would go out and party. But Brett went home to do push-ups, sit-ups, and lift weights. He performed this routine every night—not because his dad made him, but because he wanted to. Big Irv just kept him focused.

Brett Favre credits his father, Irv, for helping him to achieve success on the football field. When Brett was a child, his father made sure Brett followed a strict workout regimen that gave him an edge over other players. Brett and his father are pictured here at San Francisco's 3ComPark.

A FOOTBALL FAMILY

Partly, Brett thought he needed to work harder than most football players because he was not the most gifted athlete. Scott was a better high school quarterback than Brett, and so was Jeff. All three Favre boys played football under Irv. In fact, Irv probably would have suited up his daughter, Brandi, too, if he could have figured out a way to slip on a helmet and pads and get her onto the field without anyone noticing. (In those days, girls did not play football in school, unless it was powder puff.) However, there was little chance of sneaking Brandi through the locker room without any of the boys taking notice. She was too pretty. As a teenager, she won Miss Teen Mississippi.

The Favre family pretty much ate, drank, and slept football. During breakfast, they would talk football. On the way to the high school, they talked more football. With both parents being high school teachers, the whole family rode together to school. The family spent so much time together—school, football practice, nightly workouts—they formed an unbreakable bond. Brett also developed strict self-discipline and a strong commitment to football. Being part of a family who also loved the sport made those qualities easy to adopt.

Irv coached the boys to be tough football players. As Brett reveals in his autobiography, Irv would tell the kids, "If you get hurt, get off the field. If you can't crawl off the field, then I'll come out and get you. But don't give me any of that crybaby stuff where you're acting as if you're dying out there. Don't pretend you're hurt when you're really not because you won't get any sympathy from me." To Irv, football was a physically demanding sport. Brett learned how to be tough from his dad. Even when he got hit hard, he would get back up.

Heading into his sophomore season, Brett was excited to play for his dad. Unfortunately, he found out he had mononucleosis after just the second day of practice. His spleen was enlarged from the disease. If Brett got hit, his spleen could rupture, and he would bleed to death. At that time, Brett did not even know what a spleen was. But he knew what the news meant—he would be out for the season. Surprisingly, being sidelined for the season turned out to be a good thing. Brett was a skinny kid, weighing only 160 pounds (73 kilograms). With nothing else to do but work out and eat Bonita's home cooking, Brett packed on about 25 pounds (11.3 kilograms). Also, his bout with mono made him realize just how much football meant to him. It was torture watching from the sidelines. Brett never wanted to go through that agony again. By the start of his junior year, Brett was itching to get back on the field.

Years later when Ty Detmer was Favre's **backup** in Green Bay, they got to talking about high school football. Detmer told Favre that he had thrown for around 8,000 yards in high school. Favre had only thrown for 800 yards total. However, his small number of passing yards was because his coach did not like to call many passing plays. Irv ran a **wishbone offense** for most of his coaching career, even though he knew Brett could throw the ball. Before Irv started coaching at Hancock, the Hawks were not very good. During one streak, the team lost 36 straight games. And many of these losses were not close, either; they were blowouts, with scores such as 71-0. When Irv took over as head coach in 1972, he decided to try something different. Instead of going toe-to-toe with teams, the Hawks would run an offense that gave them more options. The wishbone offense worked well, and he stuck with it.

During Brett's junior year, Irv switched to a Wing-T offense. In the **T formation**, Brett only got to throw the football about six or seven times a game. But his team won. The Hawks went 6–4 during Brett's junior year and 8–2 his senior year. Brett doubted they could have done any better if he had thrown more. The team had two players rush for 1,000 yards each, which was excellent. While Brett could throw the ball a long way, he was not a very accurate passer at that time. He had not yet developed a touch on the ball. In practice, his teammates would run short 5- or 10-yard routes, and Brett would fire the ball at them as hard as he could. Smack! The football would bounce off their chests or helmets. During one game in his junior year, Brett threw a touchdown pass so hard that when his teammate jumped up to grab it, the ball pushed him back two feet (0.6 meters).

In addition to quarterback, Brett also played safety on defense and punted. At safety, he was slower than some of his teammates, but he hit anyone who came in his path. On offense, one of his favorite plays was the 838 Power Pitch. In it, he was the lead **blocker**, and he would bulldoze any opposing player who got in his way. Brett was not assigned to a particular opponent during the play; he would just come barreling around the corner and take out any guy he saw. At six-foot-two (188 centimeters), 190 pounds (86 kilograms), his hits packed quite a punch.

MEETING DEANNA

On Scott's sixteenth birthday, Irv took the three boys to a New Orleans Saints game. While they were gone, Bonita set up for a surprise party. She had invited both the boys' and girls' basketball teams. When Irv and the boys got back, Scott was plenty surprised, and everyone had a good time. Later in the evening, though, the party broke up a bit. Kids splintered off into their own little groups. Brett noticed Deanna Tynes go outside to shoot some baskets on their basketball hoop. A year older than Brett, Deanna was a feisty guard on the girls' varsity team. In Hancock County, everybody knew everybody else. Brett already knew who Deanna was and thought she was pretty cute. Her dark brown hair and emerald eyes had caught his attention on more than one occasion.

Although it was getting dark, there was a light by the hoop. Thirteen-year-old Brett stood by the window watching her for a while. Finally, he worked up the courage to go outside and talk to her. He made some small talk while he finished a hot dog. Being typical teenagers, they were both sort of shy and embarrassed at first. But they had similar interests—they were both athletes—so that loosened up the conversation. After a while, Brett decided to try a little flirting. "If you can call taking the ball away from her flirting," he later admitted in his autobiography. He started showing off with some slam dunks.

Some time later, Scott and his girlfriend asked Brett and Deanna to go for a drive with them. They drove to the cemetery. In the backseat of the dark car, Brett's hand brushed against Deanna's. Nervous and shy, he quickly pulled it away. Later that night, he held her hand for about five long seconds and even gave her a soft kiss.

Brett and Deanna's first real date was a dance in the tiny town of Dedeaux. Although Dedeaux was barely a bump in the road, it had a big building where dances were held. Back then, those dances seemed like a huge deal to Brett. There was a DJ and they served potato chips and Cokes. However, everyone at the dances dressed casually—T-shirts and blue jeans. At Dedeaux that night, Brett and Deanna had their first dance to "Time Will Reveal," a slow song by the group Debarge.

Both being jocks, as Favre called them, Brett and Deanna had a lot in common. Deanna was named an all-conference and all-district basketball player in her junior and senior years. She also excelled at fast-pitch softball. She even took karate for three years in high school, which Brett thought could come in handy when hanging around the Favre clan. Usually, the two of them would end up playing some type of sport when they got together. Brett was a pitcher on the baseball team, and Deanna would sometimes catch for him. He would fire fastballs at her, never easing up just because she was a girl. One day, Brett's dad came storming out of the house and told Brett to stop throwing so hard. "You're going to kill that poor girl," Irv said.

Brett stopped his windup and turned to his dad. "Why?" he shouted back. "She's catching 'em, ain't she?" Her hand may have been on fire, but Brett knew she could handle it. She was just as tough as he was.

Throughout high school, Brett and Deanna were almost inseparable. They lived only about 15 miles (24 kilometers) apart and spent every night on the telephone. During those late-night conversations, they talked about their dreams for the future. Brett bragged about how he would get a football scholarship to Mississippi State or some other top university. "You know, Deanna," he would whisper, "it's going to happen. You watch. I'm going to play big-time college football."

"I know you will, Brett," Deanna would whisper. She was always his biggest fan. Brett would go on to say that he would be so good that the college's alumni would buy him a car. Then, he told her he would play professional football someday, too. Again, Deanna would agree with him. She bragged to her mom, who was a huge professional football fan, how Brett would one day be playing in the National Football League. "Mama, Brett can throw the ball eighty yards," she would say. Her mother did not believe her, though. "Don't be silly, dear," she would reply, "pro quarterbacks can't throw it that far."

FAVRE 4 SOUTHERN MISSISSIPPI

During his senior season, Brett received some interest from the big schools in the surrounding area—Auburn University in Alabama; the University of Alabama, Birmingham; the University of Mississippi; Mississippi State University; and Louisiana State University. However, his recruitment was generally limited to a form letter or an occasional visit by an assistant coach who would stop by to say hello on his way through town. None of them ever followed up on anything. To these colleges, Brett Favre was just another name at the bottom of a long list.

The only person to show genuine interest in Brett was Mark McHale, the offensive line coach at the University of Southern Mississippi in nearby Hattiesburg. Coach McHale met Irv while on a recruiting trip the summer before Favre's senior year. Naturally, they talked football and really hit it off. So they stayed in touch. Favre's senior year was much like his junior

During his senior year of high school, Brett Favre was not highly recruited as a quarterback; most colleges wanted him to play safety. However, Favre had his heart set on playing quarterback, so he decided to attend Southern Mississippi University in nearby Hattiesburg. It was there that number 4 established himself as one of the top quarterbacks in the country.

year; he continued to be a hard-hitting safety with decent range and a quarterback who ran more than he passed. He threw the ball only a few times per game, but he could hand off like a pro. Likewise, his season statistics were unimpressive—about 460 passing yards and eight touchdowns. In reality, Favre knew he would probably end up at safety in college, which was the position he played in the Mississippi High School All-Star football game in Jackson. What he really wanted to play, though, was quarterback.

Favre believed he could be a good college quarterback. The trouble was no one had ever seen him throw. By the time spring rolled around during his senior year, no four-year universities were prepared to give him a look at quarterback. The best offer came from the University of Southern Mississippi, where the coaching staff thought he would make a decent safety and **special teams** player. Favre considered going there, but he did not want to give up his dream of playing quarterback. His dad thought Brett could play quarterback in college, too. So he called Coach McHale to come down one afternoon for a visit. Technically, McHale could not conduct a private workout with Brett, because it would be a **National Collegiate Athletic Association** (NCAA) violation. But suppose McHale stopped by just to chat, Irv suggested. And suppose on the way out of Irv's office, Brett just happened to be on the practice field throwing a football. Coach McHale agreed to make the one-hour drive from Hattiesburg to take a look at Favre.

The next day, McHale dropped by Irv's office. By some *strange* coincidence, Brett just happened to be out on the practice field throwing the ball. When Coach McHale saw Brett launch a 65-yard toss, his jaw nearly hit the ground. There was no one on the entire Southern Mississippi roster who could throw the ball that far. Favre may have been presented with a scholarship offer right there on the spot, but the coaching staff at Southern Mississippi did not have any scholarships left to hand out that year.

Five days before the signing deadline, Favre weighed his options. Only three schools offered him a chance to play at quarterback—Delta State in Cleveland, Mississippi, a Division II school; Mississippi College in Clinton, Mississippi, a Division III school; and Pearl River Junior College in Poplarville, Mississippi, a two-year college. Finally, Favre decided he could go to Pearl River for two years and hope some four-year college would offer him a scholarship from there. A few days later, while babysitting for his cousins, Favre got a call from Coach McHale. He asked Favre if he wanted to play at the University of Southern Mississippi. Apparently, a player from Florida backed out and McHale had convinced the head coach to offer Favre the final scholarship. USM had six quarterbacks, so Favre would be seventh string, but that did not bother him. He gladly accepted the scholarship, because he was confident he could show the coaches how great of a quarterback he really was.

Fortunately for Favre and his freshman teammates, USM officials made it possible for them to arrive six days before the upperclassmen. This gave the players a chance to take their physicals and get their jersey numbers, and, as Favre added, find a cool place to hang out. In high school, Favre's number had been 10. It was his favorite number, and he had worn it from fifth grade through his senior season. As he recalled in his autobiography, when he asked the equipment manager for number 10, the manager explained that 10 was former quarterback Reggie Collier's number and was more than likely going to be retired. (After his days at Southern Mississippi, Collier played three years in the United States Football League (USFL) and two years in the NFL.) The team was not going to give his number to just any player. Growing up, two of Favre's heroes were Dallas Cowboys quarterback Roger Staubach and Pittsburgh Steelers quarterback Terry Bradshaw (both number 12), so next he asked for 12. But that number was taken as well. Favre thought some more. His brother Scott's number had always been 11, so he asked for that one. No, that number was already taken, too. Frustrated, Favre finally asked, "Well, what number can I have?"

The equipment manager said he had one number left—4.

"Four?" Favre said disappointedly. "I don't want 4. That's stupid."

However, there were 100 players on the roster. The equipment manager said he could take it or leave it. Well, Favre took it.

Quarterback Surprise

Freshman football players at Southern Mississippi participated in "double days" before the upperclassmen arrived on campus. Players worked on offense in the morning and defense in the afternoon. In the fall of 1987, Brett Favre did both. His goal was to make the traveling squad. The top three players at each position traveled with the team, so Favre figured he had a good chance at safety. Quarterback was another story. The roster boasted several talented quarterbacks, including Ailrick Young, Simmie Carter, David Forbes, Michael Jackson, and Jay Stokes.

Favre's first chance to show off his throwing ability came on the scout team. They were supposed to prepare the first team for the opposition, but Favre was making them look bad—completing pass after pass. His skill at quarterback turned out to be a pleasant surprise to the coaching staff. The coaches raised their eyebrows and commented, "This guy ain't bad." But he was still seventh string.

Favre's next big chance came during a game commonly called Suicide. During this scrimmage, the freshmen would battle the upperclassmen—the rookies versus the big boys. For the most part, the freshmen typically got pummeled. The freshman team's starting quarterback was Michael Jackson, who would go on to play wide receiver for eight years in the NFL with the Cleveland Browns and Baltimore Ravens. Jackson could run and throw, but he was somewhat inaccurate. After a couple of days, the coaches decided to try Favre at quarterback. He played well against the upperclassmen, throwing for two touchdowns against the number 1 defense in one scrimmage. From that day on, he worked his way up the **depth chart**. First, a couple of players got hurt. Then, the coaches moved Jackson to receiver. Suddenly, Favre was third string.

THE 1987 SEASON

The USM Golden Eagles lost their season opener, 38-6, against the University of Alabama. Still, being on the field in front of 75,000 fans at Legion Field in Birmingham was thrilling for Favre, even if it was on the sidelines. At that point, Head Coach Jim Carmody was thinking about **redshirting** Favre, which meant he would sit out his entire freshman season. However, he would still be eligible to play for four more years after that. But Favre had the feeling he just might end up playing that season.

After the Alabama loss, the Golden Eagles faced Tulane. Ailrick Young started at quarterback. He was playing OK, but Southern Mississippi was still getting beat. The coaches decided to insert Simmie Carter into the game during the second quarter, but he did not have much luck, either. At halftime, Coach McHale suggested to Coach Carmody to give Favre a chance. "Well, he can't do much worse," Carmody said.

Originally a quarterback at Southern Mississippi, Michael Jackson quickly switched to wide receiver once Brett Favre established himself as the Golden Eagles' signal caller. Jackson would go on to have a solid eight-year NFL career with the Cleveland Browns and Baltimore Ravens.

Favre worried that he might do worse. He did not really think he was going to get a chance to play in that game. So the night before, Favre and offensive lineman Chris Ryals played a drinking game called Quarters. The object of the game is to bounce a quarter into the other guy's beer glass. If the quarter bounces in, the other guy takes a drink. The guy bouncing the quarter has to take a drink if he misses the glass. Between the two of them, they drank a case and a half of beer. Needless to say, Favre was not feeling too well the next day against Tulane. It was about 110°F (43°C) in Hattiesburg, and standing on the sidelines, Favre felt as if he was going to throw up. Suddenly, Coach Carmody turned to Favre and told him that he was going into the game. Favre could hardly believe it. His adrenaline helped him shake off his hangover. He pulled on his helmet and trotted out to the huddle.

Seventeen-year-old Brett looked around at the offensive linemen. They were all seniors—21- and 22-year-olds. The Golden Eagles were losing, 17-3, but Favre's teammates believed in him. Nervous yet under control, Favre drove the team down the field on the first series. His first touchdown pass came off a **bootleg**, where the quarterback fakes one way and rolls out the other. Favre threw a balloon pass that fluttered into the hands of senior wide receiver Chris McGee. It may have been an awful-looking pass, but McGee caught it. Favre went crazy. He ran over and jumped on Coach Carmody. Luckily Carmody was excited, too, and hugged him back. Favre threw another touchdown pass that day, and the Golden Eagles rallied for a 31-24 win.

The next week, Coach McHale met with Favre and gave him some surprising news. "We're going to start you," he said, as Favre recalled in his autobiography. The Golden Eagles were scheduled to play Texas A&M in Jackson, Mississippi. Legendary coach Jackie Sherrill led the Aggies, and the Associated Press ranked his team in its Top 10. It came as little surprise when the Golden Eagles lost that day, 27-14. Still, Favre was happy. He played pretty well, well enough to earn the starting position for the rest of the season. He completed 79 of 194 passes for 1,264 yards and 15 touchdowns—a school record—and the Golden Eagles finished 6–5. All in all, it was not too shabby for a seventh-string quarterback.

(continues on page 43)

TEENAGE PARENTS

During the summer before Brett Favre's sophomore year of college, Deanna delivered some startling news. She was pregnant. They reacted the same way any young couple would—they were scared. Favre tried to concentrate on football, but it was tough for him. Instead of acting like himself—happy and carefree—he became serious. Millions of thoughts fluttered in his mind. Would he have to quit school? Was his football career over? Where would he get a job to support the baby? Not surprisingly, he did not play well during fall camp. He threw as if he was distracted. His reads were not sharp, and the passes flew all over the place.

From time to time, Irv drove up to Hattiesburg from Kiln to watch Brett practice. It did not take him long to figure out something was wrong. He suspected that Deanna was pregnant but figured Brett would tell him when he was ready. One weekend when Brett was home, he and Deanna split up with Brett's parents. Brett sat in the living room with his dad while Deanna went off somewhere else with his mom. Not wanting to prolong the silence, Brett just blurted it out. Irv did not say a word. He just got up, walked into the kitchen, and started doing the dishes. Brett knew his dad was upset, because Irv always did the dishes when he was bothered by something.

Back in high school, Irv had warned Brett about this type of situation. "I know you really like that girl," he would say, "but whatever you do, don't go getting her in trouble." Of course, Irv meant not to get her pregnant. Now, Brett had done exactly what his father had told him not to do. After Irv finished cleaning the dishes, he came back into the living room and sat down next to Brett. As Favre recalled in his autobiography, his father looked him in the eyes and said, "I'm not going to preach to

After a 14-year courtship, Deanna Tynes and Brett Favre finally got married on July 14, 1996. Deanna's mother, Ann (left), and Brett's mother, Bonita (right), are also pictured here.

you. I'm not going to scold you. All I'm going to say is that I expect you to step up and be a man about this." Irv promised to do whatever he could to help out, but asserted that it was Brett's responsibility.

After telling his father, Brett felt as if a huge weight had been lifted off his shoulders. Irv wanted to know, though, what Brett and Deanna planned to do. Deanna and Bonita sat down in the living room with them, and they discussed the situation. For Brett and Deanna, abortion was not an option. They were both Catholic and against abortion. They talked about Brett dropping out of school, quitting football, and finding a job. But neither Brett nor Deanna liked that option. Naturally, they

(continues)

(continued)

bounced around the idea of marriage. Deanna, however, felt she was not ready to get married, and Brett agreed. They both had friends who had fallen into the same situation, got married too soon, and then ended up divorced two years later. Both Brett's parents and Deanna's parents thought the kids should not get married unless they were ready. So they decided to stay together as teenage parents—18 and 19—but hold off on getting married.

At first, Brett and Deanna tried living together, but that arrangement did not turn out well. They argued about silly things, like most young couples. After a while, Brett moved out but still stayed in close touch with Deanna. On February 6, 1989, daughter Brittany was born. Many nights, Brett stayed with Deanna to help take care of their baby girl. He would change diapers in the middle of the night and play football the next day. Even after he was drafted by the Atlanta Falcons in 1991, Favre would drive the old back roads after finishing practice on Friday to get to Deanna's and then drive all the way back to play on Sunday. Brett and Deanna took their time getting married. They tried dating other people but somehow always found their way back to each other. After a 14-year courtship, they finally got married on July 14, 1996, with a giddy, seven-year-old Brittany looking on. Three years later, Deanna gave birth to Breleigh on July 13, 1999—one day before their anniversary. Although she was five weeks early, both mother and baby were fine. Now together for 25 years, Brett and Deanna have created their own modern-day fairy tale, where two small-town high school sweethearts overcame many obstacles to live happily ever after.

(continued from page 39)

During his freshman year, Favre worked hard to learn the Golden Eagles' offense. They ran the **I formation** in which the **running backs** line up directly behind the quarterback. From that formation, the Golden Eagles ran a variety of plays, including the **toss sweep** and **off-tackle** running plays, mixed in with some **drop-back passing**. Naturally, Favre had little experience in the passing game. Therefore, it took some time for him to pick it up. Today, when Favre looks back, he realizes how simple it actually was. When he passed, the back would split and block for him. Years later in Green Bay, the offense was much more complex, with his receivers running many different patterns and his running backs being responsible for four or five different protections. At USM, it was basic. They would run plays like 75 XYZ Cross. The 75 was the protection, and receivers X and Y would cross on the play. Or, they would pick the 75 Right Z Hook, in which the Z receiver would run a hook. In retrospect it may have seemed simple, but for Favre—who played in the Wing-T offense in high school—it seemed rather complicated.

THE 1988 AND 1989 SEASONS

By his sophomore season, Favre had developed a strong command of the I-formation offense. The team went 10–2 under new coach Curley Hallman, including a 38-18 victory against UTEP in the Independence Bowl. Favre set a handful of single-season records—passing yards (2,271), total offense (2,256), and touchdown passes (16). In addition, he threw only five **interceptions** in 319 pass attempts for a 1.57 interception ratio—the lowest ratio in the nation for the top 50 passers. Coach Hallman was so impressed, he started promoting Favre as a Heisman Trophy candidate. He created the slogan "Favre 4 Heisman." As Favre recalled in his autobiography, Coach Hallman told reporters, "If you go back at the end of last year and look at the top players in the country, and that's what the Heisman Trophy is supposed to represent, then you have to throw

Favre's name in there with the best ten." He also added, "The mark of a truly great player is that he makes the other players around him look a little bit better. And Favre has that kind of quality about him." That year, however, Favre did not win.

Before Coach Hallman came to USM, he coached **defensive backs** at Texas A&M. He remembered Favre's good game against them in 1987. Most of all, he noticed Favre's composure. The defense continued to pressure him throughout the game, but Favre never let it get to him. Hallman could already tell that Favre was something special.

During his junior season, the Golden Eagles opened their 1989 campaign on the road against sixth-ranked Florida State. The Seminoles were stacked with talented players. Everybody in the country expected USM to lose. The Las Vegas oddsmakers listed USM as 27-point underdogs. Coming off a 10–2 season, the Golden Eagles were still flying high. Coach Hallman worked them hard in preparation for Florida State. The game took place in Jacksonville, Florida, on September 2, 1989. That day, the weather was brutally hot—more than 100°F (38°C)—and humid. In fact, the security guards at the stadium had to take approximately 100 people to the hospital for heat exhaustion.

Oddly, however, the heat turned out to be an asset for USM. Apparently, Florida State coach Bobby Bowden did not run his players much. He thought he did not need to bother because the players were so talented. The lack of conditioning took a heavy toll on the Seminoles. On defense and offense, the Golden Eagles dominated the game. Favre threw two interceptions, but he also had two touchdown passes. He completed 21 of 39 passes for 282 yards in leading the Golden Eagles to a stunning 30-26 victory. On the plane ride back to Hattiesburg, the players mimicked the Seminoles' tomahawk chop. When they got to the airport, 20,000 people were there to greet them. The team celebrated at Favre's favorite hangout—the North End Zone. Every time ESPN played highlights of the game, they would all start waving their imaginary tomahawks and chant,

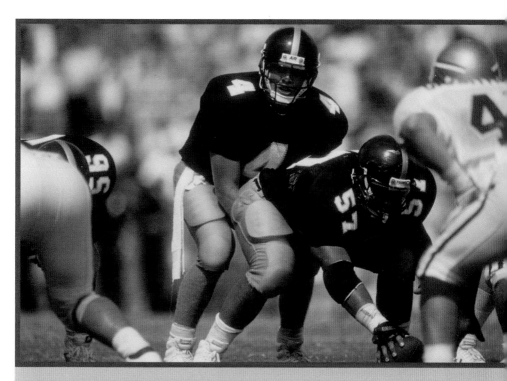

In the opening game of Brett Favre's junior season in 1989, he helped guide Southern Miss to one of the biggest wins in school history—a 30-26 victory over sixth-ranked Florida State. Favre completed 21 of 39 passes for 282 yards in the stunning win.

"Hey, oh! Hey, oh!" When the Associated Press (AP) Poll was released that Monday, USM was ranked twelfth in the nation. However, they did not stay there long. They lost their next four games and finished the season with a disappointing 5–6 record. Favre was determined to make his senior year a success.

JUST WATCH ME

In May 1990, Favre had bone spurs removed from his right elbow. Luckily, the surgeon did a fantastic job, and Favre was throwing better than ever. However, another trip to the hospital would not turn out so great. On a sunny Saturday in July, Brett, his brother Scott, and USM linebacker Keith Loescher went fishing on the Gulf of Mexico. The sun blazed the temperature to 110°F (43°C) and gave them all nasty sunburns. Just before sundown, they put their fishing poles away and headed for home. Favre planned to grab a quick shower and catch a movie with Deanna, who was playing in a softball tournament that day. He drove alone in his brand-new white Nissan Maxima. Keith and Scott followed in another car. Favre was cruising along at about 70 miles per hour, which was much faster than he should have been driving. About seven-tenths of a mile (1.1 kilometers) before he reached his parents' house, his right tire hit some loose gravel on the shoulder. He tried to straighten out the car by turning his steering wheel, but because he was going so fast, the car skidded across the road. The Maxima hit a culvert, slid down an embankment, flipped in the air three times, and slammed into a pine tree. The bumper peeled off the bark as it slid down the tree trunk. Inside the car, Favre was out cold.

Rushing up to the car, Scott could see Brett was unconscious. At first, he thought his brother was dead. Panicking, Scott grabbed a golf club and bashed in the front window to get to Brett. When Brett came to, glass was bursting everywhere. All Brett could see was broken glass and trees. Confused, Brett asked Scott if he had been in a plane crash. Favre believes the automatic seat belt saved his life. His car hit the tree with such force that the belt snapped. But instead of being thrown from the car and killed, he ended up in the backseat. Carefully, Scott and Keith slid Brett onto the road and waited for the ambulance and Brett's parents to arrive.

As Brett recalled in the book *Favre*, he repeatedly asked his mother during the drive to the hospital, "Am I going to be able to play football again?" Every bump in the road caused excruciating pain in his back. She just said, "Honey, I don't know."

In the emergency room, the doctor explained to Favre that he had a fractured vertebra, a lacerated liver, a severely bruised abdomen, and some abrasions. "There is no way you're playing football this year," he announced. The doctor's flat reply ticked

Favre off. He did not like anyone telling him what he could and could not do. "Just watch me," Favre said, as written in his autobiography, *Favre*.

The accident took a toll on Favre's body. He stayed in intensive care for three days. He could not move for a whole week. A nurse had to give him baths, and his mom and dad had to help him go to the bathroom. Five days later, however, Favre was back home recovering. The day of the accident was July 14. The season opener was just six weeks away. Favre hoped he could make it. For the next three weeks, everything seemed to be going fine. Then, his stomach started hurting again. Every time he tried to eat, he would throw the food right back up. At first, the doctors thought it was just a reaction to the trauma of the accident. But Favre insisted they take a closer look. The doctors discovered that 30 inches (76 centimeters) of Favre's intestine had been crushed and no longer functioned. With eight feet (2.4 meters) of intestine, there was no need to worry, though. The damaged section could be removed. However, the extra surgery kept Favre from playing in the season opener against Delta State.

Before the accident, Favre weighed a solid 226 pounds (103 kilograms). When he finally returned to Hattiesburg in mid-August, he weighed just 192 pounds (87 kilograms). In a few short weeks, he had lost 34 pounds (15 kilograms). "I was as weak as a kitten and skinny as a scarecrow," Favre recalled in his autobiography. Even though Favre was in no shape to play against Delta State, USM defeated them, 12-0. The next game was against thirteenth-ranked Alabama. Throughout the week, people were wondering whether or not Favre would play. Favre was still not 100 percent, but he was stronger. On the Friday before the game, Coach Hallman asked Favre if he could play. Favre gave him a confident "sure."

Hallman decided Alabama did not need to know the good news. On game day, he started John Whitcomb, a redshirt freshman, at quarterback. Then, after the first play, Favre ran onto the field. Much to Favre's surprise, 76,000 Alabama fans cheered for him. Back in the huddle, some of his teammates even had tears in their eyes.

On the first play, Favre dropped back to pass. Right after he released the ball, he got drilled, laid out flat. The entire stadium fell silent. Everyone must have thought the same thing—he busted open his stomach. Southern Mississippi's head trainer, Larry "Doc" Harrington, came running out onto the field. He leaned over Favre and asked him what was wrong. Favre was gasping for air, feeling as if he was going to throw up.

"Doc," Favre said, "I got hit in the balls."

Relieved it was not the stomach, Doc said, "Oh, good." In the book *Favre*, Brett recalled thinking, *No. Not good.* Favre made it through the injury, but not before the Alabama fans realized what had happened and had a little chuckle over it. They were not laughing for long, though. Golden Eagles place kicker Jim Taylor nailed field goals from 45 and 53 yards. A senior safety returned an interception for a 75-yard touchdown. And Tony Smith, the Golden Eagles' running back, ran for two touchdowns. Alabama may have outgained USM 442

FAVRE'S CAREER PASSING STATS AT SOUTHERN MISSISSIPPI

YEAR	GP	C/A/I*	PCT.	YDS.	TD	YD./ATT.	YD./COMP
1987	10	79/194/13	.407	1,264	15	6.5	16.0
1988	11	178/319/5	.558	2,271	16	7.1	12.8
1989	11	206/381/10	.541	2,588	14	6.8	12.6
1990	10	150/275/6	.541	1,572	7	5.7	10.5
TOTALS	42	613/1,169/34	.512	7,695	52	6.5	13.0

*=completions/attempts/interceptions

yards to 195 yards in total offense, but the Golden Eagles still upset the Crimson Tide, 27-24. Favre was **sacked** twice in the game, but pulled through.

Favre rallied back from his injury to have a good senior season. The following week, USM played at the University of Georgia. With two minutes left in the game, the Bulldogs were leading the Golden Eagles, 18-17. Favre drove the USM offense to the Georgia 25-yard line with 54 seconds left in the game. Taylor attempted a 42-yard field goal, but the ball clanged off the right goalpost and bounced back onto the field. The loss did not bring the team down, though. They won four of their next five games before losing to Virginia Tech, 20-16, in Blacksburg, Virginia. USM finished the regular season with an 8–3 record, good enough to earn a berth in the All-American Bowl. Although they lost to North Carolina State, 31-27, Favre was named the game's Most Valuable Player after throwing for 341 yards and three touchdowns. After the season, he was invited to play in both the Senior Bowl and the East-West Shrine game, where he was named Most Valuable Player.

Although he never won the Heisman Trophy, Favre proved that he was one of the best players in the country. Favre finished his career at Southern Mississippi with several school records, including passing yards (7,695), pass attempts (1,169), completions (613), **completion percentage** (51 percent), and touchdowns (52). However, Favre was most proud of his career interception ratio of 2.9, which ranked among the all-time best in NCAA history.

During his final season at USM, there were a lot more people watching him than just the doctor who told him he would not play football that season. Several NFL teams considered Favre a fairly high draft pick. However, they wanted to take a look at him up close, so Favre held a predraft workout in Hattiesburg. Approximately 20 coaches and scouts showed up, including Seattle Seahawks assistant coach Ken Meyer,

After his senior season at Southern Mississippi, Brett Favre held a predraft workout for NFL scouts and coaches. One of the NFL coaches in attendance that day was June Jones of the Atlanta Falcons. Jones was instrumental in convincing the Falcons to take Favre with the 33rd overall pick in the 1991 NFL draft.

Atlanta Falcons assistant coach June Jones, Los Angeles Raiders assistant coach Mike White, and San Francisco 49ers assistant coach Mike Holmgren. Favre felt he had put on a pretty good workout, launching throws and demonstrating his agility. All of the coaches and scouts said hello to him, but Holmgren was the only one who actually took the time to sit down and chat with him. The 49ers were not looking for a quarterback, he told

THE HEISMAN TROPHY

Born on October 23, 1869, John William Heisman grew up around the oil fields of northwestern Pennsylvania in the town of Titusville. The first football games he played in were a hodge-podge of soccer and rugby. In 1887, at the age of 17, Heisman left Titusville for Brown University. There, he played a form of club football with his classmates. Two years later, he transferred to the University of Pennsylvania to pursue a law degree. Although he was just 5-feet-8-inches (173 centimeters) tall and 158 pounds (72 kilograms), he played varsity football for three years as **guard**, center, tackle, and sometimes tight end.

After a flash of lightning nearly blinded him, he took his final exams orally and graduated with a law degree in the spring of 1892. Immediately after college, he accepted a coaching job at Oberlin College. It was only the second year of Oberlin's football program, but he led the team to a perfect 7–0 season. Heisman enjoyed similar success at Auburn, Clemson, Georgia Tech, the University of Pennsylvania, and Rice. His most impressive coaching stint was at Georgia Tech, where, from 1904 to 1919, he posted a record of 102–29–7. During one stretch, Heisman coached the Golden Tornado to an astounding 33-game unbeaten streak. (Georgia Tech outscored its opponents 1,599 to 99 during the streak, including a 222-0 win over Tennessee's Cumberland College.) After the 1919 season, he left Georgia Tech to return to the University of Pennsylvania as head coach. Three years later, he bought out his contract, spent a year at Washington and Jefferson College, then moved west to Houston, Texas, where he closed out his career at Rice Institute. In a coaching career that spanned 36 years, Heisman changed the face of football. Noted for a number of innovations, includ-

(continues)

(continued)

ing the center snap, his greatest contribution may have been to help legalize the forward pass.

After his coaching days, Heisman became the first athletic director of the Downtown Athletic Club (DAC) of New York City. There, he founded the Touchdown Club of New York and later the National Football Coaches Association. While he was with the DAC, he created a voting system to determine the best college football player in the country. However, he inwardly opposed recognizing an individual over a team. The first Downtown Athletic Club Trophy was presented to the University of Chicago's Jay Berwanger in 1935. In early October 1936, before the second award could be presented, Heisman died of pneumonia. When the trophy was presented to Yale's Larry Kelley two months later, the officers at the DAC had renamed the award the Heisman Trophy, in honor of one of the most influential men in college football history.

Favre. They already had Joe Montana, Steve Young, and Steve Bono. But for future reference, Holmgren wanted to work Favre out and see for himself what this young quarterback with the amazing arm could do. He assured Favre that he would probably be picked early in the draft.

As the 1991 draft drew closer, several reports circulated about who would pick Favre. Atlanta quarterbacks coach June Jones said he believed the Falcons would take Favre with the thirteenth overall pick. They had the fifth, thirteenth, and thirty-third picks. A scout with the New Orleans Saints thought perhaps Favre might go in the top 15. However, he added, he did not think Favre did a good enough job of moving out of the pocket to go that early. "Shoot," Favre later commented in the book *Favre*, "that's what I do best."

Finally, draft day arrived. Favre was pretty nervous, hoping to be picked early, maybe in the top 15. Picks came and went. The Falcons took Mike Pritchard, a receiver from Colorado, with the thirteenth pick. Team after team passed on Favre, and by the end of the first round, he still had not been drafted. At this point, Favre was becoming agitated. A number of teams assured him that they would take him in the first round. Finally, Atlanta took him in the second round, with the thirty-third overall pick. Although he was drafted after San Diego State quarterback Dan McGwire and USC quarterback Todd Marinovich—two signal callers who would go on to have lackluster NFL careers—Favre was relieved when the Falcons finally selected him. He was ready to play pro football.

Storybook Beginning

Everyone talks about storybook endings. Brett Favre had what some people might call a storybook beginning—it just took a year to happen. His rookie season as a third-string quarterback with the Atlanta Falcons was anything but magical. He was sacked once and did not complete a single pass to a teammate in his four pass attempts (although he did complete two passes to the opposition). In his book *Favre*, he said, "It's hard to be that bad without trying." Fortunately, all that bad luck was soon to change.

During his first off-season in 1992, Favre stayed at his parents' pool house on their Mississippi property. One day in February, Irv Favre delivered a message to his son that the general manager of the Green Bay Packers, Ron Wolf, had called. Favre was supposed to return the phone call as soon as possible. Immediately,

Favre worried that he might have been traded. The thought ticked him off a little. He felt that Atlanta had given up on him too soon.

When Favre called Wolf, he received some unexpected news. Wolf explained that he had traded a first-round pick to Atlanta for Favre. He believed Favre could be the Packers' quarterback of the future. In any case, he was willing to give Favre a chance. Wolf thought Mike Holmgren, the new head coach, would be the perfect mentor. Favre, Wolf said, was a born leader, a player who had the potential to be more than just a **starter**. But he would have to buckle down and work hard. Most important, Favre had to want it more than anything else in the world.

Favre was excited to be working with Coach Holmgren. In San Francisco, Holmgren had worked with quarterback greats Joe Montana and Steve Young. Undoubtedly, he could shape Favre into a better quarterback. The apprenticeship would have its rough spots, though. There were times when Holmgren did not like something Favre would do in practice or in an exhibition game. Burning with anger, Holmgren would walk right past Favre in the hallway without saying a word. He knew that, if he started talking to Favre, he would end up yelling.

Instead, Holmgren saved his yelling for the practice field. At first, Favre was inconsistent. He had not played much in Atlanta, so basically he was still a rookie. The Green Bay offense was extremely difficult to run, especially for a 22-year-old. But Holmgren stayed on the young quarterback. Years later, Favre admitted that he could hardly blame Holmgren for pushing him so hard. He needed the motivation. He also knew that Holmgren's tough words would make him into the quarterback he always wanted to be. Even though Favre was inconsistent, however, Holmgren named him the backup quarterback, behind Don Majkowski.

In 1992, San Francisco 49ers offensive coordinator Mike Holmgren was named head coach of the Green Bay Packers. During his time in San Francisco, Holmgren had mentored NFL Hall of Fame quarterback Joe Montana, who is pictured here with Holmgren before a game with the Dallas Cowboys in November 1990.

KING OF COMEBACKS

Don Majkowski's nickname was "Majik." He led the Packers to a number of comeback wins in 1989. He also set a Packers record with 4,318 yards passing, which also led the NFL that season. In 1990, Majkowski tore his rotator cuff in the tenth game of the season and had a difficult time recovering from the injury. Although he played in 1991, he was slow to recover. During the first off-season minicamp in 1992, Majik was still unable to throw with his usual velocity. However, he was an accurate passer and knew the offense. Favre admired the way Majkowski took charge in the huddle. During training camp, Majkowski's arm strength improved. Even though Favre had begun to become more consistent, it was obvious Majkowski would be the starting quarterback.

In the 1992 season opener at Lambeau Field, the Packers lost to the Minnesota Vikings, 23-20, in overtime. Then, the Buccaneers delivered a 31-3 blowout in Week Two in Tampa, Florida, as Favre saw some playing time in the second half. No one blamed Majkowski for the losses. Along with everyone else, Favre expected Holmgren to stick with his starting quarterback.

An opportunity presented itself, however, when Majkowski tore a ligament in his left ankle midway through the first quarter of Green Bay's game with Cincinnati. When Majkowski reached the sideline, he told Holmgren that he had heard something pop. Holmgren turned to Favre and said, "You're in."

Out on the field, Favre was nervous, and it showed. His passes were all over the place. The game against the Bengals was his first real chance in a pressure situation. After all, against Tampa Bay the game had long been decided when he came in. He wanted to do well at Lambeau Field but got off to a rough start. During the Packers' first 10 **drives**, they only gained about 150 yards. And Favre had completed less than half of his passes. He **fumbled** four times and was sacked five times. But his teammates stuck with him.

Halfway through the fourth quarter, the Bengals were ahead, 20-10. Their **secondary** was sitting back in **zone**

coverage, probably thinking there was no way Favre could beat them, and they were only rushing their four linemen. The relaxed coverage gave Favre time to complete short passes, **move the chains**, and gain confidence. On a single drive, the Packers went 88 yards. Then, Favre hit wide receiver Sterling Sharpe on a five-yard touchdown pass. The Packers were now only down by a field goal, 20-17.

The Bengals had a 2–0 record coming into the game, and they were determined to make it 3–0. On the next drive, they answered with a field goal to move ahead by six points, 23-17. Things got worse for the Packers when Robert Brooks had trouble handling the **kickoff**. He panicked, picked the ball up, and stepped out-of-bounds at the Packers' 8-yard line. The Packers needed a touchdown to win. They would have to drive 92 yards with a little more than a minute left to play. To make matters worse, they had used up all their time-outs.

Favre was not about to give up. On the first play, he completed a pass to Harry Sydney, the **fullback**, for a short gain out of the **backfield**. Some fans booed Favre, because they wanted to see him throw deep down the field. But Holmgren had his own reasons for calling the short passes. He wanted to see what the Bengals' defense would do. Sure enough, they stayed in zone coverage, a **cover two** defense.

The best place to attack a cover two is deep and outside along the sideline, between the cornerback and the safety. So the Packers attacked right in this seam. On second down, Favre threw a high, hard pass to Sterling Sharpe, who made a 42-yard **reception**. Sharpe had moved behind the cornerback, and the safety came over too late to make a play. However, the safety had plenty of time to drill Sharpe in the ribs. The hit knocked him out of the game, putting even more pressure on Favre and the Packers' offense.

Even after that pass, the Bengals continued to stay in the same defense. Favre was amazed that the Bengals did not think he could beat them with his arm. The next play was a screen pass to running back Vince Workman out of the back-field. That play picked up 11 yards and a **first down** at the Cincinnati 35-yard line. By this time, there were only 19 seconds left on the clock. The Packers called a 2 Jet All Go, a play in which all four receivers go deep, and the quarterback tries to find the open receiver. Wide receivers Robert Brooks and Sanjay Beach split out wide left and tight end Jackie Harris lined up on the right side of the line. Wide receiver Kitrick Taylor, who replaced Sharpe, was wide right.

For some reason, the cornerback opposite Taylor did not bump him at the line. In this defensive strategy, a defensive player bumps the receiver at the **line of scrimmage** to slow him down. As a result, Favre had enough time to pump fake, which froze the safety for a second and created an open seam for Taylor. Favre was terrified as he threw the pass. After the ball left his hand, he closed his eyes and waited for a cheer. Moments later, Taylor caught the football as he crossed the goal line with 13 seconds to play. Favre had led the team to its first fourth-quarter comeback win under his command, 24-23. The crowd at Lambeau Field went crazy, and so did Favre. He started running around the field looking for people to hug. When he got to 300-pound guard Ron Hallstrom, the two players head-butted. The hit split Favre's forehead open, but he was too elated to care.

After that day, Favre realized there was no way he would ever be satisfied sitting on the bench. He had way too much fun on the field. He knew he belonged in the game. Holmgren said little after the Packers' win. He was proud of Favre but told him that he still had a long way to go. Favre knew he was right.

The week after the win against the Bengals, Favre made his first NFL start as the Packers beat Pittsburgh, 17-3. In the game, he completed 14 of 19 passes for 210 yards and two touchdowns. During one play, Favre used a pump fake to fool Rod Woodson, the Steelers' All-Pro cornerback. Sterling

Brett Favre walks off the field after his first career start in the NFL, a 17-3 victory against the Pittsburgh Steelers on September 27, 1992. For Favre, the game marked the beginning of a remarkable streak—through the 2007 season, he had started in an NFL record 253 consecutive games.

Sharpe caught the pass for a 76-yard touchdown. Favre was so excited that he ran down the field and jumped on Sharpe. After a couple of weeks of this excitable behavior, Favre was called into Holmgren's office. Holmgren was worried Favre might hurt one of his teammates during his "celebration" jumps. If he pulled the stunt again, he would be fined $5,000. After that, Favre tried to behave on the field.

With Favre as starter, the Packers were 8–5 in 1992, finishing 9–7 overall—their second-best record during the previous

20 years. Favre's storybook beginning as the Green Bay Packers' quarterback was a fitting start to his career. During his football career, he has become a king of comebacks. Through the 2006 season, Favre had mounted 36 game-winning comebacks in the fourth quarter or overtime. Perhaps the Packers' most important come-from-behind win came later in that 1992 season, against All-Pro **defensive end** Reggie White and the Philadelphia Eagles. On November 15, 1992, the Packers played the Eagles at Milwaukee County Stadium. That year, the Eagles were considered one of the NFL's best teams. Their defense was *the* best in the NFL, and Favre quickly found out why in the first half of the game.

White, a future Green Bay Packer, hit Favre so hard that Favre slightly separated his left shoulder. Although the pain was intense, Favre continued to play. The Packers ended up coming back to win the game, 27-24. During that off-season, White would join the green and gold. He admitted that Favre's performance in the November game was a factor in his signing. White said he thought Favre had what it took to get to a Super Bowl, and he liked Favre's toughness. With White's help, the Packers' defense would go from being ranked 23 in the NFL in yards allowed to number two in 1993. Ranking second all time in career quarterback sacks, White would be a force to be reckoned with, and Favre would be glad that he did not have to face the fearsome defensive end. The Brett Favre–Reggie White combination ushered in a new era for the Green Bay Packers. With a punishing defense and an explosive offense, the Packers would be headed for the top.

FAVRE AND HOLMGREN

Coach Holmgren demanded a lot from Favre. From 1992 to 1994, Favre and Holmgren had their fair share of run-ins. Favre was baffled at his inconsistency, and his up-and-down performance frustrated his coach, too. Holmgren is an intelligent, highly regimented coach, who runs disciplined practices and rarely jokes around. He expects his quarterback to get the play right the first time, and Favre was falling short of his expectations. By comparison, Atlanta's offense was a cinch to catch on to. The Green Bay playbook was a foot thick, with terminology that was unique to the **West Coast offense**. For example, one play was called Brown Right Slot A Right 2 Jet

BRETT FAVRE'S
36 GAME-WINNING COMEBACKS*

During his NFL career, Brett Favre has led the Green Bay Packers to 36 game-winning comebacks in the fourth quarter or overtime. Entering the 2007 season, the three-time NFL MVP ranked third all time, behind former Denver Broncos quarterback John Elway and former Miami Dolphins quarterback Dan Marino, in this category.

NO.	DATE	OPPONENT	FINAL SCORE
36	December 21, 2006	Minnesota	9-7
35	December 11, 2005	Detroit	16-13 (OT)
34	December 24, 2004	Minnesota	34-31
33	December 12, 2004	Detroit	16-13
32	November 21, 2004	Houston	16-13
31	November 14, 2004	Minnesota	34-31
30	January 4, 2004	Seattle	33-27
29	December 14, 2003	at San Diego	38-21
28	November 16, 2003	at Tampa Bay	20-13
27	November 2, 2003	at Minnesota	30-27
26	December 8, 2002	Minnesota	26-22
25	September 29, 2002	Carolina	17-14
24	September 8, 2002	Atlanta	37-34
23	January 13, 2002	San Francisco	25-15
22	December 30, 2001	Minnesota	24-13

Dino Wash All Across. Another play was Brown Lift Tight Close F Right Sprint Solid Quick Drag. There were hundreds of these types of plays to learn. Just when Favre thought he had grasped the offense, Holmgren would change things up. Favre would have to relearn it, backwards. Plus, he constantly had to read the defense and apply it to the play. Years later, Holmgren

NO.	DATE	OPPONENT	FINAL SCORE
21	December 3, 2001	at Jacksonville	28-21
20	December 24, 2000	Tampa Bay	17-14
19	November 6, 2000	Minnesota	26-20
18	October 15, 2000	San Francisco	31-28
17	September 17, 2000	Philadelphia	6-3
16	October 10, 1999	Tampa Bay	26-23
15	September 26, 1999	Minnesota	23-20
14	September 12, 1999	Oakland	28-24
13	December 27, 1998	at Chicago	13-13
12	November 1, 1998	Seattle	36-22
11	October 14, 1996	San Francisco	23-20
10	November 12, 1995	Chicago	35-28
9	December 18, 1994	Atlanta	21-17
8	October 9, 1994	Los Angeles (Rams)	24-17
7	January 8, 1994	at Detroit	28-24
6	November 28, 1993	Tampa Bay	13-10
5	November 21, 1993	Detroit	26-17
4	November 14, 1993	at New Orleans	19-17
3	November 29, 1992	Tampa Bay	19-14
2	November 15, 1992	Philadelphia	27-24
1	September 20, 1992	Cincinnati	24-23

* From the fourth quarter to tie or win (through the 2006 season)

The 1992 season brought many ups and downs for Brett Favre. Although he was sacked 34 times, including this one by Detroit Lions defensive lineman George Jamison, Favre posted an 8–5 record as a starter and established new Green Bay records for single-season passing percentage (64.12 percent) and most consecutive 200-yard passing games (11).

could toss out a new play and Favre would have no problems grasping it. But when he was starting out, it was a nightmare.

At times, Favre really struggled. He would call an off-the-wall **audible**, and the play would not even come close to being a completion. Favre would trot to the sidelines, and Holmgren would ask if he had any clue of what he just did. Trying to cover his tracks, Favre would respond that he thought he saw something. "Well, Brett," Holmgren barked, as quoted in Favre's autobiography, "in this game you can't think you saw something. You've got to see it."

Young quarterbacks often think they see a **blitz** coming when in reality the defense is in normal coverage. Holmgren calls it "seeing ghosts." Favre saw quite a few ghosts his first year as quarterback.

Holmgren would scream at Favre in practice every day, cursing and complaining. Favre got pretty embarrassed in front of his teammates. The routine reamings were having an effect on his ego. Favre wanted to do it his way. He thought he knew better than Holmgren, and for this reason, the two often clashed. Eventually, though, Favre realized that Holmgren had to be hard on him in order to make him a better player. It took a couple of years, but quarterback and coach finally warmed up to each other.

In 1992, Favre had some success, mostly due to the fact that the defense laid back and just waited for him to make a mistake. He did not make too many, though. He threw for 3,227 yards and 18 touchdown passes, with only 13 interceptions, a good enough season to be selected to his first Pro Bowl. At 23, Favre became the youngest quarterback to earn a trip to the end-of-season game in Hawaii. He set Green Bay franchise records for completion percentage (64.12 percent) and most consecutive 200-yard passing games (11).

Learning the Ropes

During the 1993 season, opposing defenses were not going to sit back in soft coverage and allow Brett Favre to pick them apart. Defenses started attacking him, blitzing like crazy. Favre's confidence was rattled, and he started making big mistakes. He threw 24 interceptions in 1993, dropping his quarterback rating to 72.2—a career low until 2005. The Green Bay fans were disappointed. They expected a repeat of 1992. In Wisconsin, fans had been waiting 25 long years for a winner. Besides, when players make large sums of money, fans expect them to perform well. Even if it did not look like it, though, Favre was trying hard. The fans just did not understand that Favre was doing his best. Moreover, he was learning on the fly, in front of 70,000 fans, and his mistakes were replayed over and over in front of him.

The 1993 season was a roller-coaster ride of wins and losses. There were good games followed by bad games followed by good games. In fact, the last six games went win, loss, win, loss, win, loss. Favre was walking a fine line between failure and success. He performed that tightrope act for two and a half seasons, struggling to achieve consistency. The Packers lost their regular-season finale against Detroit, 30-20. Favre threw four interceptions in the game, and the loss cost Green Bay the **National Football Conference** (NFC) Central Division title. All of the Packers were frustrated, especially Favre. However, the Pack managed to pull out a 9–7 record for the season, good enough to make the playoffs. They were the first Packers team since 1972 to make the playoffs during a nonstrike season. Also, it was the first time Green Bay had back-to-back winning seasons since 1966 and 1967.

The next week, the Packers were back in Detroit for the first round of the playoffs and some revenge. With less than one minute to play, Green Bay was down, 24-21. From the Lions' 40-yard line, Favre called Red Left 25 Okey Double Squareouts. The play would put Sterling Sharpe out on the left side. After the snap, Favre dropped back and looked left for Sharpe, but being tired from the previous play, Sharpe had stayed on the right side of the field. Detroit had rolled up the cornerbacks in double coverage. Therefore, Favre could not throw an out. (In this situation, the receivers are supposed to adjust and run fade routes.) With only seconds to wait, Favre continued scanning the field. He looked for tight end Ed West in the middle, but he was covered, too. Then, Favre noticed the safety was cheating way inside of Sharpe. The defender did not think Favre could throw the ball behind him. Favre thought differently. He fired the pass to Sharpe, who was wide open up the right sideline behind the safety. The touchdown delivered a 28-24 win for Green Bay.

Revenge was sweet, but the Packers had to play again the following week. Their reward: a trip to Texas to play the defending Super Bowl champion Dallas Cowboys in the divisional round of the playoffs. Although Favre played pretty well, completing 28 of 45 passes for 331 yards and two touchdowns, Green Bay lost to Dallas, 27-17. After the game in the

FROZEN TUNDRA FANS

The motto of Packers fans is, "The colder the better." They revel in the frigid weather and wear it like a badge of honor. Even in below-zero wind chills, Packers fans show up at Lambeau Field two hours before kickoff. They come in their blaze orange hunting gear, snowmobile suits, or long johns and jeans to tailgate and party. When the game begins, they cheer like mad and stay to the bitter cold end.

Lambeau Field has been dubbed "The Frozen Tundra." Oftentimes, it feels just like it sounds. Still, Brett Favre's record in cold weather (below 34°F, 1°C) stood at 40 wins and 5 losses through the 2006 season. In these games, he has completed 890 of 1,441 passes for 10,242 yards, 79 touchdowns, and a passer rating of 90.7. So how can a quarterback from southern Mississippi play so well in cold weather? Favre says it is due to the fans. Because the fans feed off the cold weather, so do the players. They do not care if there is freezing rain, icy roads, or six feet (1.8 meters) of snow on the ground. If they have to go to work in the hazardous conditions on Monday morning, they can sure get to the game on Sunday afternoon.

More than anywhere else, Green Bay fans feel as if they are part of the team. In fact, they own it. The Packers are the only publicly owned, nonprofit team in football. The team has about 2,000 stockholders, and not one of them makes a dime. There are stockholders in every state in the country and even in three foreign countries. Unlike other teams in the league, the Packers know they will always be in Green Bay. Throughout the rest of

locker room, some of the guys acted pleased that they had only lost by 10 points. But Favre hated to lose, even if it was by only one point. Although he knew the Packers still had a long way to

the league, owners can threaten to move the team somewhere else if the team is not bringing in enough revenue or they do not get the stadium deal they want. According to Packers bylaws, if for some odd reason the Packers had to be sold, the money would go to Green Bay's Sullivan-Wallen American Legion Post.

People in Wisconsin treat the Packers the way they treat their high school team. Green Bay is the smallest city that has an NFL team. The fans grew up with the Packers. Favre has had grown men come up to him and tell stories about cheering for the Packers when they were three years old. The team is part of who they are. Around town, one does not have to look very far to see something that has to do with football. Kids go to Lombardi Middle School and residents drive down Lombardi Avenue. (Vince Lombardi was a famous football coach in the 1960s, who led the Packers to victory in the first two Super Bowls.) The stadium is named after Curly Lambeau, who not only established the team, but also served as a player and coach. There are hundreds of businesses in the area with the word *Packers* in their names, such as Packer City Antiques, Packerland Kennel, and even Packerland Chiropractic.

Lambeau Field has been sold out each season since 1960, and on game day, the fans still rock the stadium. As many as 40,000 fans show up just for scrimmages. It can be 100°F (38°C) or 5°F (-15°C) —and sunny, rainy, or snowy. The weather does not matter to Green Bay fans; only that their beloved Packers are playing football.

Brett Favre trots off the field after the Packers' 28-24 win against the Detroit Lions in the first round of the NFL playoffs on January 8, 1994. The playoff victory was the first for the Packers since the 1982 season.

go before they could be as good as Dallas, Favre was not about to settle for anything less.

ONE GOAL

In 1994, Favre was convinced the Packers were going to take the next step. However, the team hit a few bumps early on. Once again, the team was up and down. One week, Favre would be on fire—calling the right plays and running them perfectly. The next week, the Packers would not be able to overcome their mistakes and would end up losing. The season nearly came to an end for Favre in Week Eight at Minnesota. He took a nasty hit in the first quarter. Favre tried to keep playing, but he had suffered a bruised hip and could barely walk. Finally, he had to be replaced by Mark Brunell. At half-time, Favre told Holmgren that he thought he could go back in. But Holmgren stuck with Brunell.

At that moment, Favre thought perhaps he was finished; that Brunell would be the guy to play the rest of the season. Even if Favre could make great plays, he was inconsistent. During practice, games, and even after games, Holmgren was in his face. And when he was not on Favre's case, he was pulling his hair out on the sidelines. The Packers lost to Minnesota, 13-10, in overtime, and their record dropped to 3–4.

The next day, Favre met with Steve Mariucci, the quarterbacks coach. He validated Favre's worst fear with blunt honesty—Holmgren was thinking about replacing him. A couple of the assistant coaches also felt the same way. Favre was not too surprised. In practice, the coaches had been somewhat cold to him. If Favre made a play, no one said anything. But if Brunell did, they would all congratulate him. However, Mariucci supported Favre, and Holmgren agreed to stick with him as quarterback. Now it was up to Favre to make something out of his second chance.

Perhaps Holmgren was just trying to get Favre fired up. Maybe it was a lesson in reverse psychology—a way to force Favre to be more focused, to work harder. One thing was certain—it got Favre's attention. The game against the Vikings was on a Thursday night, so the Packers had that weekend off. Favre went home to Mississippi, where he did a lot of intense soul searching. When he left Mississippi, he had only one goal: He was going to be the best quarterback in the NFL.

The fact that he was benched during the Minnesota game served to inspire Favre. After the game against the Vikings, he was a different quarterback. Everything just seemed to fall into place for him. He saw the field much clearer, became more familiar with his opponents, and began realizing why some plays worked and others did not. During the first two and a

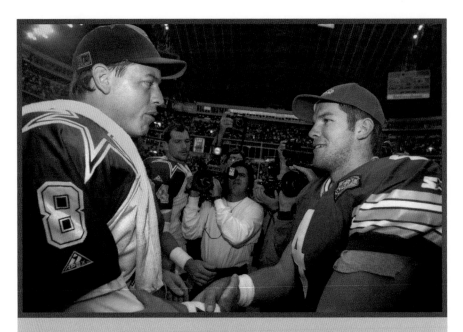

Brett Favre offers congratulations to Dallas quarterback Troy Aikman after the Packers lost to the Cowboys, 35-9, in the divisional round of the NFC playoffs on January 8, 1995. The win by the Cowboys was the second of three straight over the Packers in the playoffs.

half seasons of his career (up to the Minnesota game), Favre held a 21–17 won-lost record with 46 touchdown passes, 44 interceptions, and a 78.5 passer rating. During the next two and a half seasons (after the Minnesota game), his statistics catapulted to a 30–11 record with 101 touchdown passes, 33 interceptions, and a 98.4 passer rating. The change in Favre was astounding. The Packers won seven out of their next 10 games, including a 16-12 victory over Detroit in the **wild-card** round of the playoffs. This time, the Lions came to Lambeau Field. The Packers' defense held Detroit running back Barry Sanders to negative yardage. During that game, Favre felt the Packers were finally coming together as a team. However, the two-time defending Super Bowl champion Cowboys once again stood in their way. And once again, Dallas beat Green Bay; this time by the score of 35-9.

LEADER OF THE PACK

For Favre, the 1994 season offered another crucial transformation as well. That year, he became the true leader of the offense. Until then, Sterling Sharpe had worn the crown. However, during training camp, Favre had finally dared to challenge him. He had just signed a four-year, $19 million contract extension in the off-season, and Sharpe was jealous. One day in practice, Favre threw two passes in a row to Sharpe—one high, the other low. Sharpe trotted back to the huddle and muttered, "For $19 million, you ought to be able to put it right on my hands." According to his autobiography, Favre—furious by the comment—shouted back, "Shut up and catch the ball." The huddle fell uncomfortably silent. For a moment, Favre thought maybe a fight would break out. But Sharpe did not say another word. He just crouched down with the rest of the players and listened for the next play.

Midway through the season, Sharpe suffered a hamstring injury. He could barely run well enough to play in games. Even though Sharpe's production declined, the Packers were still winning games. More comfortable with the offense by this time, Favre was just throwing to whoever was open. During one game, Coach Holmgren asked Favre if he was upset with Sharpe. He assumed Favre was throwing to other players on purpose—something Favre would never do. Holmgren told Favre to try to work Sharpe back into the game a bit. Although they lost to Buffalo, Dallas, and Detroit, Sharpe caught six touchdown passes in those three games. So, obviously Favre was able to get him back into the game. His amazing finish to the 1994 season set the stage for an incredible season in 1995.

One of Favre's fondest football memories of the 1995 season took place during a 35-13 win against Tampa Bay in Week 13. The Packers were inside the Buccaneers' 10-yard line. This particular play was supposed to be a rollout right and a toss to tight end Mark Chmura in the corner of the end zone. However, Chmura got knocked down at the line of scrimmage. Another quarterback might have thrown the ball away and tried his luck during the next down. Not Favre. As he spun to his left, he caught a glimpse of wide receiver Robert Brooks at the back of the end zone. He threw the ball across his body. The pass barely made it over one defender and in front of two others, but it connected for a touchdown. When Favre reached the sideline, Holmgren grabbed him and asked if he knew what he was doing out there. Favre said he did. Then Holmgren said, "That was the best play I've ever seen in my life." This type of risky play is what often brings criticism to Favre's game. Throughout his career, Favre has been considered a gunslinger and has been criticized for taking too many chances; oftentimes he believes that he can connect on any throw. Many critics believe Favre uses poor judgment at times. After all, during the 2007 season, he broke George Blanda's NFL record for career interceptions. Blanda threw 277 during his 26-year career. But others argue that Favre's riverboat gambler attitude is what sets him apart and makes him a great player. In essence, one has to take the good with the bad.

FIRST MVP AWARD

Favre set the league on fire in 1995. He threw for 4,413 yards (a league high) and 38 touchdowns to win the NFL's Most Valuable Player Award. Plays like the one against Tampa Bay helped him earn MVP honors. In addition, Favre led the NFC with his 99.5 passer rating and set a new Packers record with seven 300-yard passing games. As a team, Green Bay finished the regular season 11–5 and won its first NFC Central Division title since 1972. In the wild-card round of the playoffs against Atlanta, Green Bay scorched the Falcons, 37-20.

After that game, Favre walked off the field thinking one thing—he hoped they would play San Francisco next. The 49ers were the defending Super Bowl champions and Holmgren's old team. Favre knew it would be thrilling for the Packers to knock them out of the playoffs. Sure enough, the Pack went out to play

The 1995 season was a turning point for the Packers; they won their first NFC Central Division title since 1972 and advanced all the way to the NFC Championship Game. Here, Brett Favre runs off the field after the Packers' 24-19 win against the Pittsburgh Steelers on December 24, which clinched the division title.

San Francisco. Favre had one of his best games yet, completing 15 of 16 passes in the first half. He finished the game with 299 yards passing and two touchdowns, and a 27-17 victory that no one thought was possible.

The moment of glory was short-lived, however. For the next playoff game, the Packers traveled to Texas Stadium, where they once again had to face their nemesis, the Dallas Cowboys. Going into the fourth quarter, the Packers were leading, 27-24. Green Bay was only a quarter away from playing in its first Super Bowl since the 1967 season. Unfortunately, the Cowboys had other plans. Dallas running back Emmitt Smith capped a 90-yard drive with his second touchdown of the game to give the Cowboys a 31-27 lead. Favre then threw an untimely interception that set up another Smith touchdown run that sealed the win for Dallas, 38-27. The 1995 season was over.

In his book *Favre*, Brett explained what Holmgren told him after the San Francisco game: "I'm proud of you. We've come a long way. We're going to be in this for the long haul." For the first time, Favre finally felt as if he belonged. He was accepted, and people believed in him. Holmgren had given him a chance, and Favre had taken advantage of it. To Favre, it felt as if he had cleared a huge hurdle in his life. However, a new type of pressure quickly moved in and filled its place.

The Addict

In his autobiography, Brett Favre wrote, "I know just about everything there is to know about painkillers. . . . Percodan. Lortab. Vicodin. You name it, I've swallowed it." He could rattle off labels of recommended doses and side effects. When it came to getting "Vikes," as he called Vicodin, he could name the who, what, where, when, and how. However, Favre warns that there is nothing glamorous or sophisticated about being an addict. In Green Bay, he became one.

After his first couple of years in the league, Favre thought he was bulletproof. His addiction to the painkiller Vicodin only inflated that illusion, and for two years, it dominated his life. At the height of his addiction in 1995, he would lie, beg, or borrow for his Vikes. Even though he knew pill-popping was wrong, it was hard to beat the addiction. Vicodin is a powerful, highly addictive narcotic. The drug delivers a sense of euphoria—peace, happiness, and contentment—to the user. Depending on how many pills a person takes, the buzz can last several hours or longer. Unlike alcohol, there is no hangover or sluggishness the next day. The pills were Favre's security blanket, his escape, and his obsession. Whatever he was doing, Vicodin helped him enjoy it more. He planned every weeknight around those pills.

DEALING WITH THE PAIN

Favre's first experience with painkillers came during his sophomore year at Southern Mississippi. After his elbow surgery, the doctor gave him a prescription for Vicodin, Percodan, or Lortab—all painkillers. Favre just took a few pills for the pain, and that was it. Then, after his car accident before his senior year, he got another prescription. Again, he only took the pills when he felt pain, as he was supposed to do. He never saw anyone at USM popping painkillers in college. During his rookie year in Atlanta, he did not know of anyone taking painkillers, and he really never thought much about them.

During his first season with Green Bay, Favre came to realize what all NFL quarterbacks have to deal with week in and week out. They are heroes one day and sore the next. Once the adrenaline from the game wears off, the pain sets in. During the game against the Eagles that season, Favre was repeatedly knocked to the ground and sacked twice. On one hit, future teammate Reggie White slammed his 300-pound frame into Favre. As Favre's left shoulder smacked into the turf, it separated. Even though he was in pain, he toughed it out and kept playing. At halftime, he got an injection of Novocain, which numbed the shoulder. It was enough to get by, but Favre still felt pain every time he threw the football.

After that game, Favre took Vicodin. At first, he popped a couple pills just to help him get through the rigors of the grueling NFL schedule. Then, he started taking them for a buzz. Eventually, he became addicted, and by the end of the 1994

During his first season with the Green Bay Packers, Brett Favre began to take Vicodin to alleviate the pain he experienced by being knocked down so often. In his Green Bay debut against Tampa Bay, Favre was sacked four times, including this one by Buccaneer defensive tackle Santana Dotson.

season, he was taking six a day. During the worst period of his addiction, he got into a routine where he would pop as many as 15 pills at nine each night. He had a lot of trouble swallowing the long, bitter, gritty pills. He would toss them in his mouth and force them down with a big gulp of water. Usually, he would throw them back up. Favre would simply pick the pills out of the vomit, rinse them off, and try again. When he finally got them all down, the buzz would kick in. He would sit up watching late-night television or play video games. Those days, he only slept a few hours a night. The more pills he took, the less tired he became.

However, taking that many pills tore up his stomach. Most nights, he would suddenly have to run out the back door and throw up on the sidewalk. Deanna, who was living with him at the time, would sometimes hear him and come downstairs. She would ask what was wrong, and Favre would tell her he just did not feel well. Other nights, she would sleep right through it. Favre was not eating much. And he was so horribly dehydrated that the skin on his lips, face, hands, and arms was flakey and chapped. He would drink bottled water by the gallon but hardly went to the bathroom. He even became so constipated once before a game that he had to have an emergency enema.

Favre commented on how it was a wonder he ever won the NFL MVP Award in 1995. He was in such sad shape. However, he never took painkillers before or during a game. It is a myth that players pop pills before a game in order to play with pain, he asserts. If he had taken three or four Vikes before a game, it would have been impossible for him to throw the ball accurately. He would have gotten clobbered on the field. Favre had to be clearheaded and on his toes. There was no way he could have run an offense with a buzz.

MOVING TOWARD ADDICTION

Favre's pill-popping addiction evolved slowly. During his first three seasons, he would get banged around a bit and afterward ask one of the team doctors for a couple of pain pills. Team doctors keep a strict record of injuries. So, they would ask Favre where he hurt, jot it down, and hand him two or three pain pills. Favre also kept an eye on teammates who got injured. If someone got six pills, Favre would stop him in the locker room and ask to borrow a couple. Most often, his teammates were more than happy to share a couple pills with the quarterback if he was in pain. At first, Favre was not taking many and not every night. It was easy to build up a supply, and he did not have to scrounge around for pills.

During his first two seasons in Green Bay, he would stop taking Vicodin in the off-season. He packed his bags and headed to Diamondhead, a resort area near the Mississippi Gulf Coast, where he rented a house. There, he did not think about painkillers. He was too busy playing golf and hanging out with his brothers and buddies. Late in the 1994 season, that all started to change. By that time, he had fallen victim to serious drug abuse. No longer did he just want the pills, he needed them. After losing to Dallas in the divisional playoffs, Favre headed for Mississippi, this time with a bottle of 30 Vicodin. Taking six a night, this supply would not have lasted very long. But while he was home, he needed hernia surgery. The doctor placed plastic mesh in Favre's side so the torn muscle would heal. Meanwhile, the recovery was painful. This time, he had a legitimate pipeline to large quantities of Vicodin. About a month after the surgery, he really did not need the pills anymore. But he kept taking them anyway. He would pretend to be in a lot of pain so that the doctor would write him another prescription. Before long, Favre was popping 8 to 10 pills a night.

Just before the 1995 season, Deanna and Brittany, who was six years old at the time, moved to Green Bay to be with Favre. Deanna and Brett were not yet married, but they had decided it was time to try to make it work. The three of them moved into a four-bedroom house on the west side of town, about five minutes from Lambeau Field. Everything seemed to be going great, but it was only on the surface. Deanna had no idea that Brett was addicted to painkillers. For a while, he kept it a secret. Eventually, however, there was no way to hide his addiction.

Favre's pill-popping routine had always been very disciplined. On weekdays, he would come home from practice, take a nap, get up, and start watching the clock for 9:00 P.M. to roll around. He would wait until nine at night to take the pills, because that way, the buzz would last until he went to sleep—about three in the morning. He never took Vicodin two days before a game, only after a game and on Monday through Thursday. The more pills he took each night, though, the more effort he had to put into getting the drugs. He covered his tracks well. He never relied on just one person to supply him. In fact, it is likely that none of the people Favre went to even knew he or she was contributing to a drug problem.

There were times he asked Deanna to call her dentist and complain about a toothache to get some Vicodin. When she asked why, he said because his side was killing him and there was no other way to get any painkillers. He did the same thing with his brother Scott. He lied to team doctors, trainers, and teammates. At times, he called teammates in the middle of the night, saying he was in excruciating pain. He would then ask them if they could bring over some Vikes. Before long, Deanna began to figure things out. Favre had stopped talking about family and goals. Instead, he stayed up half the night watching television, surfing the Internet, or playing Sega golf. He went through horrible mood swings. He left pill bottles lying around the house. Most of them were not labeled, but one day Deanna found one that said Vicodin. It all started making sense to her.

Deanna started keeping track of bottles. Each day, she counted pills. Either a lot of pills were missing or the bottle was completely empty. Finally, in November 1995, she confronted Favre. He refused to admit he was abusing painkillers. Instead, he distanced himself from Deanna. He had to avoid her in order to keep his secret buried. Deanna tried to talk to Favre's parents about the problem, but they found it hard to believe. Favre had fooled almost everyone around him— teammates, coaches, and friends. His dedication could not be questioned. He showed up early, worked out hard, and attended every team meeting. From time to time, he dozed off during the afternoon quarterbacks meeting. Coach Mariucci would elbow him in the side to wake him up but thought nothing of it—lots of players were tired after working out all day. Besides, Favre still did not miss a beat. He would go home and study really hard before taking his pills.

FAVRE SLIPS UP

Two weeks after the 1995 season, though, Favre started to do a poor job of concealing his addiction. He and Deanna flew to Hawaii for the Pro Bowl. They had a lot of fun that week, spending time with Favre's agent, James "Bus" Cook, his wife, and Scott and his girlfriend. Favre did not play much in the game, but he felt tired and worn-out afterward. The group had about four hours to kill before their flight home, so they sat down by the pool and began partying. After drinking only two beers, Favre felt as if he was ready to pass out, he was so exhausted. So he went up to his room and popped 15 painkillers—a combination of Lortabs, Vicodins, Percodans, and Tylenol 3. Soon, he was flying high.

On the flight home, it was obvious to Favre's friends that he had taken something. He would not stop jabbering to the woman sitting next to him on the plane. They flew to Los Angeles, where they switched to another plane. Favre did not remember the flight home.

Brett Favre poses with actor Dennis Hopper after Favre won the 1996 ESPY Award for best NFL player. Later that night, Deanna threatened to leave Brett after she discovered he was still popping painkillers.

A week later, he and Deanna flew to New York City for the ESPY Awards. ESPN was honoring Favre as the NFL player of the year. "If they only knew," Favre later commented. Everything went smoothly for the first part of the night. Actor Dennis Hopper presented the award to Favre. During his acceptance speech, Favre had a bottle of Vicodin tucked in his pants pocket. Later that night, he decided to pop it open. He excused himself from the table and was gone for an hour trying to swallow the pills. He finally got them down and returned to the party, where he began posing for photographs and talking to everyone around him. When he got back to the table, Deanna could see what he had done. She decided that she had put up with it long enough. Not long after the party, she told Favre if things did not change, she was moving back to Mississippi and getting on with her life.

At first, Favre did not believe Deanna. He continued popping painkillers. But by this time, his brother and Bus had begun to confront him, too. Even Favre's dad finally called the Packers' doctors and talked to them. Favre knew it was time to stop. He flushed the pill bottle down the toilet and never took another painkiller again. It took some time to bounce back, but before too long, Favre was starting to feel and act like himself. He and Deanna again talked about their future, his appetite improved, and he began thinking about all the goals he wanted to accomplish in football. Kicking his Vicodin addiction seemed almost easy. A few weeks later, however, Favre found out it would be much harder than he originally thought.

REHABILITATION

In late February 1996, Favre flew to Green Bay to have surgery on his left ankle. One of the team doctors was going to remove a bone spur and some bone chips—a routine procedure. The Packers' physicians had scheduled the operation for February 27. That way, Favre could play in the Pro Bowl and still be healthy for the postdraft minicamp in April. The surgery went smoothly. The only wrinkle occurred when the anesthesia made Favre vomit, but the doctor assured him that was a fairly common reaction.

In a private room on the second floor of Green Bay's Bellin Hospital, Brett, Deanna, and Brittany waited out his recovery. Favre was having some trouble with his IV, so he called in the nurse. He hated needles to begin with, and the back of his hand was swollen and sore. When the nurse arrived, Brittany was stretched out beside Brett in the hospital bed, flipping through television channels with the remote control. Deanna sat at the foot of the bed. The nurse lifted Favre's hand and started to pull out the needle. Brett glanced over at Deanna and rolled his eyes, relating how much he hated this stuff. Then, just as if someone had turned out the lights, everything went black.

What happened next Favre later learned from Deanna. Suddenly, his eyes rolled back into his head. His arms and legs started thrashing around, and his head snapped back. He started gnashing his teeth, and Deanna worried he might swallow his tongue. She screamed at the nurse to grab Favre's tongue before he swallowed it. By this time, little Brittany was crying hysterically. Deanna scooped her up and took her out of the room.

When Favre finally opened his eyes, the doctor was standing over him. He told Favre that he had just suffered a seizure. It was a serious setback. People can die from seizures. The first thing that entered Favre's mind was the Vicodin. Had the painkillers somehow caused the seizure? Had he done permanent damage to his body? Right at that moment, Favre decided to come clean. He told the doctors everything about the painkillers—how he had abused them and how he had recently quit taking them.

During the second week of March, Favre met with some league-appointed doctors in Chicago. Both Favre and his doctor thought the league doctors would be able to shed some light on what had caused his seizure. However, the meeting turned out to be a type of intervention. The doctors were counselors, more interested in Favre's drinking habits and drug abuse than in his seizure. By the end of the session, the counselors told him that he was addicted to painkillers and probably had a drinking problem, too. They referred Favre to the Menninger

Clinic, a drug and alcohol rehabilitation center in Topeka, Kansas.

Favre was floored by the assessment. "Thanks, but no thanks," he told them. After all, he was the NFL's Most Valuable Player. Surely, someone would find out about his being in rehab. If news of his stay at Menninger got out, the media would broadcast it everywhere. Besides, he had stopped taking the pills, and he did not drink much anymore. He could not understand why he would need to go to rehab.

Three weeks later, the doctors contacted Favre again. They explained that he needed to meet with an independent doctor for a second opinion. Not liking what the league doctors had to say, Favre thought this was a good idea. In New Orleans, he retold the whole story of his addiction to another doctor. He assured her that he had overcome his addiction. In his book *Favre*, Brett remembered what she said: "Well, you think you are, but you never really are." Then, she told him that she thought he needed to go to the Menninger Clinic, too. Favre left the office feeling frustrated and cornered. He thought he had been doing everything right—working out, spending more time with Deanna and Brittany. Why was everyone against him?

Meanwhile, Favre had visited two neurologists who assured him that the Vicodin had not triggered the seizure. They believed it could have been caused by one of several things. During the 1995 season, Favre had suffered three concussions, which could have sparked a seizure. Or, perhaps the lack of sleep while he was still on Vicodin or the nasty reaction to the anesthesia could have had something to do with it. In any case, the odds of him suffering another seizure were pretty small. That news put Favre's mind at ease. At this time, he was also busy putting together his first charity golf outing—the Brett Favre Celebrity Golf Tournament. It was to be held on May 17–18 in Gulfport, Mississippi. With only a couple weeks to go,

Favre was frantically calling sponsors, teammates, and players around the league.

Then, he got another call from one of the league's doctors. He flatly told Favre that he was "in the program," and he needed to go to Topeka. Apparently, the league had classified Favre's drug addiction as behavioral-referred, rather than self-referred, because the Packers' team doctors had contacted the league about it. In reality, Favre was the one who had revealed his addiction to painkillers, not the Packers' doctors. But that did not matter to the league. He would report to the Menninger Clinic or be fined four weeks' pay, which was about $900,000.

Still, Favre tried to get out of going. But it was no use. In the end, he did not want to do anything that might get him suspended for the upcoming season. He knew the Packers had a shot at winning the Super Bowl. Finally, he agreed to go. First, though, he decided to tell Mike Holmgren about the situation. The league's substance-abuse program is confidential, so even though the team doctors knew about Favre's addiction, Coach Holmgren and General Manager Ron Wolf had no idea.

The news stunned Holmgren, but he did not panic. He decided the best way to handle the situation was to hold a press conference and tell the public. The plan made sense to Favre. He would have to miss at least one minicamp, if not two. Sooner or later, reporters would start asking questions. If they fished around enough, they would find out. Favre decided it was better to be up front about the rehab. The Packers' public relations staff prepared a statement for Favre to read to the media. While he told reporters about his drug addiction and rehab, he was so nervous his leg began shaking uncontrollably. Luckily, he was standing behind a podium, so no one noticed. "They'd have thought I was having a seizure on the spot or maybe withdrawals right there in front of them," he later commented in *Favre*.

The first Brett Favre Celebrity Golf Tournament took place without its host, two days after Favre checked into the Menninger Clinic. There, Favre's home was a 12-by-12-foot room with a twin bed, couch, desk, and a jack to plug in a telephone. The telephone could be checked out at the front desk for 15 minutes at a time. Still, Favre had a lot of freedom to

THE MENNINGER CLINIC

The Menninger Clinic is ranked as one of the nation's top psychiatric hospitals. Founded in Topeka, Kansas, by three brothers—Drs. C. F., Karl, and Will Menninger—in 1925, it was the first group psychiatry practice. The clinic was revolutionary in its approach to medical illnesses. At that time, people with mental illnesses were either cared for by their families or placed in an asylum. The Menninger Clinic was a symbol of hope. The three founders gathered together a psychiatric staff dedicated to helping people who were struggling with disorders that interfered with their quality of daily life.

Since the clinic opened in 1925, the staff has helped more than 250,000 patients in the United States and throughout the world. The Menninger approach addresses multiple areas of care—medical, psychological, and familial. Each day, the clinic deals with various areas of need, including mood disorders such as depression, obsessive-compulsive disorders, eating disorders, and substance abuse. In 2003, the clinic was relocated from its original home in Topeka to a beautiful 14-acre facility in Houston, Texas. The clinic consists of seven buildings, including a dormitory-like residence hall, a separate dining hall, a school, and a gym. Outside, residents can play tennis, enjoy a dip in the pool, or take a jog on the fitness trail.

move around the clinic. Every morning, he got up at 7:00 A.M. and did 50 push-ups and 100 sit-ups. Then, he would go for a three-mile (4.8-kilometer) run and hit the gym. He played racquetball and basketball against a 50-year-old trainer named Roger. When Favre first got there, Roger could easily beat him. Before long, though, Favre started to get in better shape. He was eating right, exercising, and drinking only water. When Mike Holmgren visited him at the clinic, he could not believe how great Favre looked.

In addition to his improved physical condition, Favre experienced other positives at Menninger. Favre was going to daily psychotherapy sessions. During these meetings, he realized that he had treated Deanna pretty unfairly over the years. Whenever he experienced success, he would push her to the side and celebrate with his teammates. But when he was sick or down in the dumps, he would lean on Deanna. The therapist helped Favre to see that he either needed to marry Deanna or give her a break and let her go. Favre could not imagine life without Deanna. She and Brittany were the best things ever to happen to him. He decided he wanted to marry her. Every time Deanna called or visited, he would ask her to marry him. At first, she said nothing because she did not know if he was serious. But when Favre got out of the clinic, she could tell he had changed. Her old Brett was back. Finally, she said yes.

On July 1, 1996, Favre showed up at team headquarters on Lombardi Avenue in Green Bay. Everyone on the team welcomed him back. Later that month, on the first day of training camp, the Packers held another press conference. This time, Favre was more relaxed. While he was at the Menninger Clinic, he learned how to talk about his addiction. After he was finished speaking, reporters began shouting out questions. In his autobiography, Favre remembered that one reporter asked him if he was worried about suffering a relapse. Favre

Brett Favre answers questions from the media after returning from his 46-day rehab stint at the Menninger Clinic in Topeka, Kansas. During the press conference, Favre challenged anyone to bet against him. In 1996, he not only overcame his addiction to painkillers, but he would also lead the Packers to a place they had not been in nearly 30 years.

confidently answered, "No." But he could see doubt in the reporter's eyes. "All I can tell people is if you don't believe me, bet against me," Favre continued. "But eventually, you'll lose. I'm going to beat this thing. I'm going to win the Super Bowl." Favre had made his prediction. Now, he had to make it come true.

Super Bowl Bound

After rehab, Brett Favre had a fresh perspective and renewed energy when it came to football. A couple days into training camp, he had more confidence than he ever had. When Favre looked back on his NFL career—despite some speed bumps along the way—each year had brought him a step closer to his ultimate goal: the Super Bowl. The first year, the Packers had a winning season. Then, the second and third years, they made the playoffs. The fourth season, they came within one game of reaching the Super Bowl. For Favre, the 1996 season would surely be the year he would take that final step. He was determined to get to the Super Bowl.

The 1996 season was all about the team. The Packers had built up a strong defense to match their potent offense. Favre did not care how well the Packers' stiffest competition—Dallas or San Francisco—played. What mattered to him was how the Packers performed on the field. If they could split their road games and win at home, they would secure home-field advantage in the playoffs. And nobody could beat the Pack at Lambeau Field, Favre said.

A GREAT START

Green Bay opened its regular season in Tampa Bay. Favre was confident that the Packers would beat the Buccaneers. His premonition turned out to be right on the money. The offense clicked, and Favre read the defense perfectly and delivered precise passes. He threw four touchdown passes, three of them to tight end Keith Jackson. And he was sacked only once. The Pack throttled Tampa Bay, 34-3.

In game two, Philadelphia came to Lambeau Field for Green Bay's first Monday night home game in 10 years. In the stands, the rabid "cheesehead" fans were pumped. The Pack delivered a worthy performance, beating the Eagles, 39-13. The following week, they pummeled the San Diego Chargers, 42-10. In the first three games of the season, the Packers had outscored their opponents, 115–26. They were off to a great start.

Next, the Packers were scheduled to play the Minnesota Vikings at the Metrodome in Minneapolis. Coach Holmgren had not won a game in Minnesota since he had come to Green Bay in 1992. This season was no different. The Vikings' defense pounded Favre, sacking him seven times and forcing four **turnovers**. At the end of a frustrating game, the Packers had lost, 30-21. After the defeat, Favre was fuming, but he figured they would beat the Vikings the next time they played them—the last game of the season at Lambeau Field. Of course, Favre never thought the Packers would win all 16 regular-season games. Holmgren, too, voiced this reality to the team after the game. Favre recalled what Holmgren said in *Favre*: "Losses are going to happen. We may lose again."

Although the 1996 regular season was the Packers' most successful campaign in 30 years, the team was not perfect. Green Bay started out 3–0 but suffered a disappointing 30-21 loss to the Minnesota Vikings in Week 4. In the loss, Favre was sacked a season-high seven times, including this one by Vikings defensive tackle John Randle.

The Packers made a swift recovery. The next week, they beat Seattle, 31-10, then the Bears, 37-6. Favre was back on top of his game, leading the Packers' offense to new heights. In a Monday night game against the 49ers the following week, Favre connected with Don Beebe on 11 passes for 220 yards. In the third quarter, Beebe scored on a controversial play. San Francisco safety Merton Hanks gave Beebe about a 10-yard cushion. Favre launched a pass, and Beebe dove for it. He caught the ball on the ground, and it looked as if Hanks

THE ICE BOWL

The 1967 NFL Championship between the Green Bay Packers and the Dallas Cowboys became more commonly, and more appropriately, known as the Ice Bowl. The matchup took place on December 31 at Lambeau Field with game-time temperatures dipping to a frigid -13°F (-25°C) and a wind chill around -48°F (-44°C). Nonetheless, more than 70,000 parka-wrapped, loyal Packers fans filled the stadium to watch Green Bay claim its third consecutive NFL title with a 21-17 victory.

Packers fans thought Green Bay had a distinct advantage over their opponents from the South. When the Packers took an early 14-0 lead, the fans must have been convinced they were right. However, the frigid weather took a toll on the Packers as well. Dallas scored a touchdown and a field goal with the help of two Packers fumbles to close the Green Bay lead to 14-10 heading into halftime. The Cowboys then took the lead in the fourth quarter on a 50-yard touchdown pass.

With 4:50 left in the game, the Packers trailed 17-14. However, future Hall of Fame quarterback Bart Starr kept his cool

touched him while he was down. But Beebe popped up and ran it in for a touchdown. The Packers ended up winning in overtime, 23-20.

Green Bay won a couple more games against Tampa Bay and Detroit, to improve to 8–1, before back-to-back losses to Kansas City and Dallas. The losses did not surprise Favre, though. Some of the Packers' key players had been hurt in previous games, including their best receiver, Robert Brooks. Team morale had begun to sag. It took a couple of weeks, but the

and moved the **chains.** Thanks to the temperature, which had now plummeted to -18°F (-28°C), it was easy to do. With 16 seconds to play, the Packers were less than a yard away from scoring a touchdown. After two running plays that went nowhere, Starr called a time-out. A completed pass would certainly win the game. At least an **incomplete pass** would stop the clock, allowing the Packers to set up for a field goal to tie the game and send it into overtime. Starr consulted with Coach Vince Lombardi and returned to the huddle.

Starr took the snap from center Ken Bowman. Then, Bowman and guard Jerry Kramer teamed up to take out Dallas tackle Jethro Pugh. With Pugh out of the picture, Starr dove in for an amazing and unexpected final touchdown. The spectacular finish became one of the most famous plays in Packers history. Packers fans would not get the chance to attend a playoff game in this type of frigid weather again until they watched Brett Favre lead Green Bay to a 30-13 win over the Carolina Panthers in the 1996 NFC Championship Game.

team finally got healthy again. The Pack then geared up for the stretch drive. After their losses to the Chiefs and the Cowboys, the Packers boasted an 8–3 record. They bounced back from the Dallas loss with a 24-9 victory against the St. Louis Rams. Then, they beat Chicago, 28-17, and hammered Denver, 41-6. The Packers finished out the regular season with a 31-3 win against Detroit and got their revenge against the Vikings, 38-10.

THE RUN THROUGH THE PLAYOFFS

By virtue of their league-best record of 13–3, Favre and the Packers got their wish—home-field advantage throughout the playoffs. For the first time in 62 years, the Packers had posted an unbeaten record at home (8–0). They had earned their second-straight NFC Central Division title, which the Packers had not accomplished since Vince Lombardi was head coach in the 1960s. In addition, the team scored more points on offense (456) than any other team in the league. On defense, they allowed the fewest points (210). The last team to accomplish that feat had been the undefeated Miami Dolphins in 1972. Favre also broke his own NFC record for touchdown passes in a season, throwing for 39 touchdowns on the way to his second-straight NFL MVP Award.

The Packers were rewarded with a date with San Francisco in the first round of the playoffs. The game conditions were any-thing but pleasant—temperatures were around 35°F (2°C) with a mix of rain and snow. The weather disappointed Favre because he knew it meant that the Packers would focus on their ground game. He had hoped to throw the ball 40 times in that game, but due to the inclement weather, he would not get the chance. Favre described the football that day as a "greased watermelon." His hands were so frozen he could barely grip the ball. However, he still completed 11 of 15 passes, and the Packers only turned the ball over once in their convincing 35-14 win.

The next day, Dallas played Carolina. Whoever won the game would play the Packers next. Bus and Deanna were

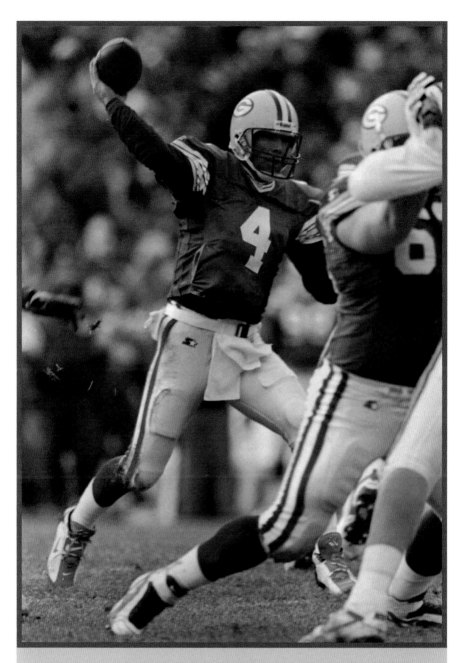

In the Packers' 30-13 win against the Carolina Panthers in the NFC Championship Game on January 12, 1997, Brett Favre completed 19 of 29 passes for 292 yards and two touchdowns. With the win, the Packers would be making their first appearance in the Super Bowl since 1968.

cheering for the Panthers, but Favre did not care who won. He was confident that the Packers could not be beaten at home. In the end, Carolina won, 26-17, setting up one of the biggest games in Packers history since the Ice Bowl.

Before the NFC Championship Game, Favre felt nervous but confident. Mostly, he was just anxious to get back on the field. He reviewed the 15 scripted plays for the game and gave the receivers a pep talk, reminding them to keep a tight grip on the ball. It was going to be cold out there—8°F (-13°C). The chilly winds did not faze the Packers. Despite the cold weather, Favre completed 19 of 29 passes for 292 yards and two touchdowns en route to an easy 30-13 victory. After a long 29-year wait, the Packers were heading to Super Bowl XXXI.

After the win against Carolina, Coach Holmgren turned to the 70,000 fans and said, "We have a great football team and we're not finished yet." The crowd responded with wild, deafening cheers. The night was frigid, but the fans did not care. They wanted to enjoy the moment just as much as Favre and the rest of the team did. In the stands, people were crying, jumping, waving, and hugging. Standing at the podium, under the roar of the crowd, Favre enjoyed the moment. It took six months, but he had made good on his prediction. The Pack was going to the Super Bowl.

SUPER BOWL XXXI

In Las Vegas, the oddsmakers made Green Bay a two-touchdown favorite to beat the New England Patriots in Super Bowl XXXI. Those odds were pretty good considering that, at the beginning of the season, many experts questioned whether or not Favre could overcome his drug addiction and regain his old form.

After two weeks of practices and overcoming a head cold, Favre's, and the Packers', big day finally arrived. At first, the Super Bowl started out like any other road game. Favre woke up in his room at the Fairmont Hotel in New Orleans, headed downstairs, and had an omelet for breakfast. He showed up for the team meeting at 10:00 A.M., which was followed by individual group meetings. Big Irv stopped by the hotel to pick up some tickets and wish Favre good luck. At 2:30, Favre hopped the bus for the Superdome. When the bus pulled in, Favre was amazed at the number of fans gathered outside. It was a sea of green and gold, Packers fans jammed up 30 to 40 deep along the road. At that moment, Favre's heart finally started to pound. It was like a home game and Mardi Gras all rolled into one. He knew this game would be the biggest of his life.

Favre walked into the locker room three hours before kickoff, an hour earlier than a typical game. He was not crazy about all the extra time he had before the game started. He decided to kill a little bit of it by arranging the postgame victory party. He got a hold of his brother Scott, who had rented a room with a balcony at Mike Anderson's Seafood Restaurant and Oyster Bar on Bourbon Street. After he got everything lined up with his brother, he headed to the training room to get his ankles taped. Ankle taping was one of Favre's pregame rituals. Kurt Fielding, one of the assistant trainers, taped his ankles every game. When Fielding finished, he pulled out his black felt-tipped marker as he did before every game and wrote his prediction for the outcome of the game on the tape. This time, he predicted Favre would complete 24 of 35 passes for 272 yards and four touchdowns and, of course, a "W" for a win. Sometimes Fielding's predictions were so close it seemed eerie.

Brett recalled in his book *Favre*, that everything in the locker room was fairly low key until right before the team was supposed to take the field for introductions. Coach Holmgren stood up and said, "Men, this is what we've worked for since that first meeting at training camp. We're here for one reason and that's to win the Super Bowl." All the while, Favre's heart was thumping so hard it nearly jumped out of his chest. "Enjoy yourself and remember this moment forever," Holmgren continued. "Now let's get out there and *get after it.*"

Favre looked around at the group of guys standing in the locker room. Before a regular-season game, at this point, the players would be goofing around. On this day, they were quiet. Some guys were crying. Others wore proud and determined expressions.

On the sidelines, Favre worried that he might launch his first pass into the upper deck due to sheer excitement. The Packers kicked off and forced the Patriots to punt. Favre took over at the Packers' 45-yard line. They had great field position, and Favre wanted to take advantage of it. On first down, halfback Edgar Bennett ran off left tackle and picked up a yard. The next down, Favre noticed that New England's defense was preparing to blitz. On Favre's second snap of the Super Bowl, it appeared as if the Patriots were going to come after him. Favre had a decision to make: Should he audible and hope that the Patriots would still blitz, or should he stay with the play and risk being sacked? With only two seconds to decide, Favre audibled to a play called 74 Razor. In this play, wide receiver Andre Rison lined up wide left with fellow receiver Antonio Freeman in the slot on the same side of the formation. In five years, he had only audibled to this particular play five times. Three times it worked, twice it had failed. Still, it was one play the defense would not expect.

When Favre audibled, everyone on the offense focused on the play. Rison lined up across from Otis Smith—the Patriots' right cornerback—and cut past him on a hard inside move. He got about five yards behind Smith. Meanwhile, Bennett picked up the Patriots' middle linebacker, who was blitzing. Now, all Favre had to do was lay the pass in just right. Rison caught the ball in stride at New England's 20-yard line and ran into the end zone for a 54-yard touchdown. Favre went crazy. He took off his helmet and jumped around as if it was the first touchdown pass of his entire career. At the time, he did not even realize how he was reacting—instinct and the thrill of the moment had taken over. He was a little embarrassed when he saw the replay, but he could not help himself. His actions mirrored how he felt.

Before long, Green Bay was ahead 10-0. However, New England came back and scored two quick touchdowns to take a 14-10 lead heading into the second quarter. Then, early in the second quarter, wide receiver Antonio Freeman scored on an 81-yard touchdown pass from Favre—the longest play from scrimmage in Super Bowl history—to put the Packers up 17-14. Everything seemed to be clicking for the Pack—the offense, the defense, and special teams.

After Chris Jacke added a 31-yard field goal to stake the Packers to a 20-14 lead, Patriots quarterback Drew Bledsoe was intercepted by safety Mike Prior on the next possession. Green Bay started with the ball at its own 26-yard line. Favre first hit tight end Keith Jackson for 10 yards and then Freeman for another 22. Then, running back Dorsey Levens carried the ball four times for 31 yards to get the Packers down to the Patriots' 2-yard line. On first-and-goal, Favre rolled left to throw to tight end Mark Chmura. But he saw that Chmura was covered, so he took off running. Over his shoulder, Favre could see Patriots linebacker Todd Collins closing in on him. He stretched out and the ball crossed the goal line just as Collins was taking him down. Favre's touchdown put the Pack up 27-14 at the half.

After New England cut Green Bay's lead to 27-21 near the end of the third quarter, the Packers responded immediately. Packers kick returner Desmond Howard took back the ensuing kickoff a record 99 yards for a touchdown, giving Green Bay a 33-21 lead. The Packers then converted a two-point conversion to go up by two touchdowns, 35-21. Howard had the best game of his career, returning six punts for 90 yards (a Super Bowl record) and four kickoffs for 154 yards, which tied him for the Super Bowl record of 244 total return yards. This performance was good enough to earn Howard the Most Valuable Player Award for the game. Some people predicted that Favre would

Brett Favre (left), punt/kick returner Desmond Howard (center), and defensive end Reggie White (right) pose with the Lombardi Trophy after the Packers defeated the New England Patriots, 35-21. In the win, Favre completed 14 of 27 passes for 246 yards and two touchdowns, White had a team-high three sacks, and Howard was named MVP after he returned four kickoffs for 154 yards and six punts for 90 yards.

get the Super Bowl MVP Award, but he was thrilled to see Howard get it. Packers defensive end Reggie White also set a Super Bowl record with three sacks. With a final score of 35-21, the Packers became the new Super Bowl champions.

After the game, Favre felt strange. The victory seemed surreal to him—it did not quite sink in. Throughout the season, the team had worked so hard to get there. During the past several weeks, there had been so much hype over the Super Bowl. Now, suddenly, it was all over. Favre could not even cry. Perhaps after all the anticipation, it would take awhile for Favre to realize he had just been through a storybook season.

When the postgame interviews were coming to an end and the cameras were packed away, the Packers' organization threw a $20,000 victory bash at the Fairmont Hotel. Brett and Deanna stayed for a couple of hours then left for Scott's party at Mike Anderson's Seafood Restaurant and Oyster Bar. At three in the morning, Favre stood on the balcony, wearing a Green Bay fireman's helmet, tossing colored beads to Packers fans swarming the streets below. He led them in chants of "Go Pack Go" and "We're No. 1." Winning the Super Bowl in New Orleans meant a lot to Favre. He grew up only 50 miles (81 kilometers) away. No one could have ever imagined that a kid from the small town of Kiln, Mississippi, would one day win a Super Bowl.

End of an Era

In July 1997, Brett Favre signed a seven-year deal with Green Bay worth between $42 and $48 million, making him, at the time, the highest-paid player in the history of professional football. That summer, he also published his autobiography, *Favre: For the Record*, which included details about his struggles with drug addiction.

Favre and the Packers kept rolling through the 1997 season. On September 21, Favre set a career high with five touchdown passes in a single game, in a 38-32 win against the Minnesota Vikings. In December, he was awarded the NFL MVP Award, sharing the honor with Detroit Lions running back Barry Sanders. Favre became the first player in NFL history to win the award three times, and in three consecutive seasons—1995, 1996, and 1997. That season was only the second time in 41 years that two players were named MVP. (The other time was in 1960, when the award was shared by Philadelphia Eagles quarterback Norm Van Brocklin and Detroit Lions linebacker Joe Schmidt.) "I can't believe a little country kid like me has won it three times," Favre said, as quoted on the *Sports Illustrated* Web site. "Considering where I came from and how hard it was to get here, it's everything I thought it would be and then some."

For the second consecutive season, the Packers finished with a 13–3 record and won the NFC Central Division title for the third straight year. By defeating the Tampa Bay Buccaneers, 17-6, in Tampa, in Week 15, the Packers also clinched a first-round bye in the playoffs. Again in the divisional playoffs, the Packers faced Tampa Bay, which posted its first winning season in 14 years. However, if the Buccaneers wanted revenge, they were sadly disappointed. Green Bay defeated them, 21-7. On January 11, the Packers played the 49ers in the NFC Championship Game at San Francisco. Once again, Green Bay vanquished the 49ers, 23-10, earning another trip to the Super Bowl, this time in San Diego, California.

SUPER BOWL XXXII

On January 25, 1998, the Denver Broncos and the Green Bay Packers duked it out at Qualcomm Stadium in Super Bowl XXXII. On the opening drive, the defending champions marched 76 yards in just over four minutes. Favre threw a 22-yard pass to wide receiver Antonio Freeman to score the first touchdown of the game. The Broncos quickly answered with a 10-play, 58-yard drive to tie the game. Two plays later, Denver cornerback Tyrone Braxton intercepted one of Favre's passes, and after an eight-play drive, the Broncos took the lead, 14-7. After only three more plays, Broncos safety Steve Atwater forced Favre to fumble. The turnover resulted in a field goal by Denver kicker Jason Elam, bumping the Broncos' lead to 17-7. The 51-yard kick was the second-longest in Super Bowl

Brett Favre sets to throw a pass downfield during Super Bowl XXXII on January 25, 1998. The 31-24 loss to the Denver Broncos was disappointing for the Packers, who entered the game as heavy favorites.

history. After an exchange of punts, the Packers fought back. Favre orchestrated a 17-play, 95-yard drive capped by a six-yard touchdown pass to tight end Mark Chmura. The score brought the Pack within three points, at 17-14, heading into halftime.

At the beginning of the second half, things looked promising for the Packers. On the first play, cornerback Tyrone Williams forced and recovered a Denver fumble. However, the Denver defense held the Packers to just a field goal, which tied the game at 17-17. Near the end of the third quarter, Broncos quarterback John Elway led a 13-play, 92-yard drive for a touchdown, increasing the Denver lead to 24-17. For a moment, the situation looked grim for the Packers when Antonio Freeman fumbled on the kickoff return, turning the ball over to the

Broncos. But, on the next play, Packers safety Eugene Robinson intercepted an Elway pass. Four plays later, Favre hit Freeman for a 13-yard touchdown to tie the game at 24-24, with thirteen and a half minutes left in the game. After both teams each had the ball twice, the Broncos took over at the Packers' 49-yard line with just 3:27 to play. Wasting little time, the Broncos reached the Packers' 9-yard line in just two plays. Then, after a **holding** penalty pushed the Broncos back to the 18-yard line, Denver running back Terrell Davis ran for 17 yards and then gave his team the lead, 31-24, with a one-yard touchdown run.

Time was running short, but Favre was not about to give up. In only a couple of plays, the Packers waltzed to the Broncos' 35-yard line. A tie was within reach, and Favre only had 1:04 to get the job done. On first down, Favre completed a four-yard pass to Levens. The next two passes, however, were incomplete. Favre had one more chance to tie the game. Facing a fourth-and-six with just 32 seconds left to play, he hurled a pass to Chmura, but Broncos linebacker John Mobley knocked away the ball to seal the victory. The game was over. Super Bowl XXXII belonged to the Broncos.

DIMMING GLORY

In August 1998, the Packers traveled to Japan for the American Bowl. It was their first overseas game in the franchise's 80-year history. There, at the Tokyo Dome, they defeated the Kansas City Chiefs, 27-24, in a nail-biting overtime win.

The Packers finished the 1998 regular season with an 11–5 record—good for second place in the NFC Central Division, behind the 15–1 Minnesota Vikings. The Packers' record was good enough to qualify for the playoffs, where they would face the 49ers for the fourth consecutive year. Again, Favre had another stellar season in which he led the league in completions (347) and passing yards (4,212). On December 20, in a 30-22 win over Tennessee, he threw his thirtieth touchdown pass of the season. This was the fifth consecutive season that Favre had accomplished the feat, breaking Dan Marino's previous record of four.

Although the Packers had won the previous three meetings against the 49ers, San Francisco quarterback Steve Young and his teammates were determined to beat the Packers this time around. Despite completing 20 of 35 passes for 292 yards, Favre threw two costly interceptions, and the Packers turned the ball over a total of four times in what turned out to be a 30-27 loss to the 49ers. The game was Favre's first defeat in nine starts against San Francisco.

The playoff loss marked the end of an era in a way. The wild-card game was Mike Holmgren's last game as coach of the Green Bay Packers. He had accepted a position as head coach and general manager of the Seattle Seahawks. Holmgren would be replaced by one of his former assistant coaches, Ray Rhodes, who had just been let go as head coach of the Philadelphia Eagles. Also, Hall of Fame defensive end Reggie White announced his retirement. In Favre's world, football was taking a twist. He probably wondered if he, or the Packers, would ever be the same without them. In some ways, they never were.

In the 1999 season opener, the Packers played the Oakland Raiders. The game was one of Favre's most memorable comeback wins. During the first half, Favre seriously sprained his right thumb. The injury made throwing difficult, and the Packers suffered in the second half. By the fourth quarter, the Raiders were ahead 24-14. However, Favre led the Packers on an eight-play, 76-yard drive to cut the lead to three, 24-21, with 7:20 left in the game. After failing to score on their next possession, the Packers took over with just 1:51 left to play. Running the hurry-up offense to perfection, Favre led the Packers on an 82-yard drive that was capped by his one-yard touchdown pass to tight end Jeff Thomason with just 11 seconds left. Behind Favre's fourteenth fourth-quarter comeback victory, the Packers topped the Raiders, 28-24.

During the postgame interview, Favre broke into tears. For him, it was a very emotional game. Being the opening game of a new era was tough enough, but then, he had to play through an injury as well. Sadly, the rest of the season did not go so well.

The 1999 season was the first and last for Rhodes. By the end of the season, the Packers had posted an 8–8 record, the worst since Favre joined the team in 1992.

However, there were a couple of positives that came out of the 1999 season. In a 14-13 loss to the Chicago Bears on November 7, Favre broke former Philadelphia Eagles quarterback Ron Jaworski's NFL record for consecutive starts by a quarterback when he started for the 117th time in a row. In breaking the record, Favre did not lose sight of what was most important to him: "I just want to play in these games, and if the records happen, they happen," Favre said in a conference call. "The most important thing, and I don't ever want to lose sight of it, because I haven't up to this point, is leading this team to victory. . . . The other things will take care of themselves." In addition to breaking Jaworski's record, *Sporting News* listed Favre number 82 on its list of the 100 Greatest Football Players of all time.

Despite the personal accolades, Green Bay continued to struggle the following season. Even young talent and a new head coach—Mike Sherman—could not get Green Bay to the playoffs in 2000. Sherman had just three years of NFL coaching experience, and none of them were as head coach. From 1997 to 1998, he served as the Packers' tight ends and assistant offensive line coach. In 1999, he was the offensive coordinator for the Seattle Seahawks. The Packers lost their first opening-season game in five years against the New York Jets, 20-16. However, in his first season as coach, Sherman restored the Packers' home-field advantage by coaching the team to five straight wins and a 6–2 overall record at Lambeau Field. The Packers finished the season with a winning 9–7 record.

In 2001, the Packers clinched a playoff spot when they crushed the Cleveland Browns, 30-7, on December 23. Throughout the season, Green Bay had battled Chicago for the top spot in the NFC Central Division. However, in the end, the Pack fell short of winning the division—finishing with a 12–4 record to the Bears' record of 13–3. Green Bay defeated the 49ers in the wild-card playoff game, 25-15, but fell to the St. Louis Rams, 45-17,

After taking the first snap of the Packers' November 7, 1999, game with the Chicago Bears, Brett Favre holds up the game ball in recognition of his 117th consecutive start. Behind and to the right of Favre is former Philadelphia Eagles quarterback Ron Jaworski, who had held the record of 116 consecutive starts since 1984.

the following week. The loss brought an end to the 2001 season and any hopes for another trip to the Super Bowl.

At the end of the 2001 season, Favre was embroiled in a controversy. New York Giants defensive end Michael Strahan was trying to break the NFL record for most sacks in a season. When the Packers played the Giants in the regular-season finale, it appeared to most as if Favre had helped Strahan achieve the record of 22.5. During one play, Favre dropped back to pass and then **scrambled** toward Strahan's side of the field and then slid down. Strahan fell on top of him to record the easy sack. The *New York Times* accused Favre of handing the record to Strahan as if he was throwing change into a Salvation Army bucket. Even though the record may have been tainted, Strahan was voted the NFL's defensive player of the year that season.

In 2002, the Packers again finished 12–4 in the regular season. During one stretch of the season, they won seven games in a row, but their hopes of claiming home-field advantage throughout the playoffs were thwarted in a 42-17 loss to the New York Jets in the final game of the season. Despite the loss, the Packers still won the NFC North Division and earned the right to host the Atlanta Falcons in the first round of the playoffs. Heading into the game, the Packers had never lost a playoff game at Lambeau Field, and with the temperature hovering around 30°F (-1°C), there was no reason to think they would lose this game. Unfortunately, the Packers were hamstrung from the beginning, because their Pro Bowl running back, Ahman Green, and safety Darren Shaper, along with their leading receiver, Terry Glenn, were all out with injuries. Green Bay fell behind 24-0 at halftime and could not overcome five turnovers, including two Favre interceptions, in a devastating 27-7 loss.

THE TWILIGHT OF HIS CAREER AND LIFE OUTSIDE OF FOOTBALL

After Super Bowl XXXII, Favre has had little success in the playoffs. Through 2006, Green Bay has only won two of seven playoff games (since 1998), including two losses at home—the first postseason losses ever at Lambeau Field. As his career winds down, Favre's glory gradually dims. Today, the most common question Favre fields is, "When will you retire?" Still, Packers fans are happy to have him around as long as he still enjoys playing the game. In 2004, Governor Jim Doyle declared November 29 Brett Favre Day in Wisconsin to honor his 200th consecutive regular-season start. That evening in a Monday

Night Football game, the Packers beat the St. Louis Rams, 45-17, as Favre threw three touchdown passes in the game.

Outside of football, Favre has used his notoriety in both Wisconsin and Mississippi as a springboard to get involved in number of community-service projects. From an early age, he was influenced by his mother, Bonita, who was a special education teacher. Unfortunately, when Brett was growing up, here were not many extracurricular opportunities for kids with disabilities. The Special Olympics was about the only organization that organized activities for these special needs children. While other children were playing basketball and softball, these kids were left out. Favre recognized this, and because he wanted to give something back to the community, he decided to focus on disabled and disadvantaged children.

In 1996, Brett and Deanna founded the Brett Favre Fourward Foundation. Since it was established, the foundation has donated more than $3 million to a wide variety of children's charities. In Mississippi, the Favres have donated money to the Special Olympics, Make-A-Wish Foundation, Candlelights for Childhood Cancer (a support group for families of children with cancer), MHG Development Foundation (which promotes community wellness through Gulfport Memorial Hospital), Gaits to Success (therapeutic horseback riding for the mentally challenged), and Hope Haven (a home for battered women and children). In Wisconsin, some of the groups the Favres support include Rawhide Boys Ranch, Make-A-Wish Foundation, Special Olympics, Cerebral Palsy of Wisconsin, CASA of Wisconsin (an organization that supports abused and neglected children), and the UW–Whitewater athletic program for athletes in wheelchairs. They donate to the Free Spirit Riders (an equestrian program for disabled children in Fond du Lac), the Boys & Girls Club of the Fox Valley, Encompass Child Care, *Green Bay Press-Gazette* education program, and the "Give a Kid a Book" program. They also contribute to Starbright, a Children's Hospital of Wisconsin program that enables sick children to use a private, broadband computer network to create an online community of hospitalized children throughout the country. The majority of the money the Favres raise to help disadvantaged and disabled children comes through three annual events: The Brett Favre Celebrity Golf Tournament and Benefit Concert, the Brett Favre Celebrity Softball Game, and the Brett Favre Steak Dinner. The softball game, which is held in Appleton, Wisconsin, has raised nearly $900,000 during the event's eight-year history. The golf tournament and benefit concert was traditionally held in southern Mississippi but was moved north to Tunica, Mississippi, after Hurricane Katrina ravaged the Gulf region in 2005. Country singer Tim McGraw has headlined this event in the past. Finally, the steak dinner event is held annually at Brett Favre's Steakhouse in Green Bay, Wisconsin.

As Favre's career comes to an end, he will undoubtedly devote more time to his charitable organization. However, his accomplishments on the football field continue to reveal the impact Favre has had on the game. For example, during Favre's reign as the Packers' starting quarterback, Green Bay held the longest streak of nonlosing seasons (from 1992 through 2004) in the NFL with 13, which included an 8–8 record in 1999. (The all-time streak for consecutive winning seasons in the NFL is 21, set by the Dallas Cowboys from 1965 to 1985.) Unfortunately, in 2005, the streak came to an end as the Packers finished a dismal 4–12. Despite throwing for more than 3,000 yards in 2005—for a record fourteenth-straight season—Favre had a below-average year. He finished with only 20 touchdown passes and was intercepted a career-high and league-high 29 times. The loss of guards Marco Rivera and Mike Wahle, as well as injured players such as Javon Walker and Ahman Green, severely hindered the team. Favre's passer rating dropped to a single-season career low of 70.9, ranking him thirty-first in the NFL.

After 2005, many people thought Brett Favre would finally retire from football. But in April 2006, he announced that he would be playing in the upcoming season. In the opening week of the 2006 season, Favre experienced something he had never

(continues on page 118)

FAVRES FEEL THE EFFECTS OF KATRINA

On the morning of Saturday, August 27, 2005, Bonita Favre was relaxing on the porch of her home in Kiln, Mississippi, watching her grandchildren play in the yard. A clear blue sky stretched above her, and not even a whisper of wind rustled the leaves of the camellia tree just outside her front door. Already at 85 degrees, she decided it was going to be another scorcher of a day in southern Mississippi. According to reports, Hurricane Katrina was bearing down on New Orleans, just 50 miles (81 kilometers) away. Bonita knew she needed to prepare for the storm, but she was having a hard time talking herself into the task. On the lawn, Favre's aunt Karen "Kay Kay" and a friend smeared suntan lotion on their legs. "If it's coming," her friend said, "we might as well enjoy the day." The Favres had survived Hurricane Camille in 1969 and half a dozen other smaller storms along the way. They would make it through this one, too, Bonita figured.

Finally, Bonita stood up and unhooked the hanging flower pots, while her oldest son, Scott, talked to her from the rocking chair a few feet away. She reminded him that the windows of the pool house still needed to be boarded up. She wondered if she should drive into Kiln and fill up the gas tank of her Cadillac. After checking the refrigerator, she decided she would have to stop at the grocery store. She only had a few bottles of water.

The Favres could not have imagined that only two days later the raging hurricane would rip through southern Mississippi, destroy their house, and threaten their lives. Rising water had never been a concern, even though their home was bordered by the Rotten Bayou on the west and Mill Creek on the east, both of which flowed into the Jordan River. The Favre house was built on a 25-foot (8-meter) hill. Surely the floodwaters would not swell that high.

On August 29, however, Hurricane Katrina's 30-foot (9-meter) storm surge pushed floodwaters 6 to 8 feet (1.8 to 2.4 meters) high into the house. Hancock County, where Kiln is located, experienced the storm's fiercest winds, with gusts up to 140 miles (259 kilometers) per hour. When the hurricane hit the Rotten Bayou, Favre's mother, grandmother, brothers, and 12 other relatives had already gathered at the Favre homestead. As the waters started to creep into the house, Scott joked that at least now his mother could get her new floors. They thought the waters might rise three or four inches (eight to ten centimeters), but the water just would not stop. Bonita glanced over to the trophy cases filled with mementos from Brett's football career. She managed to scoop up items from the first two shelves, but she had to abandon the rest when rising water forced her to move up to the attic. Within 45 minutes, the water had risen dangerously high. All 16 people, ranging in age from seven months to 87, helped each other reach the attic, where they held hands and prayed. They even managed to save their four dogs and cat. The group thought that perhaps the water would recede quickly, as it had in other hurricanes. But it did not. They were trapped in the attic for five or six hours.

During a brief calm period, when Katrina's eye passed over the house, Scott and his brother Jeff made a lifesaving decision. They swam to the boat docked on the bayou and grabbed life jackets and seat cushions for flotation devices. They also gathered food and water supplies, plucking out any bag of chips or unopened food item that floated by. When the waters lowered to about 3 feet (0.9 meters), the group evacuated to the 12-foot (3.6-meter) loft in the pool house.

(continues)

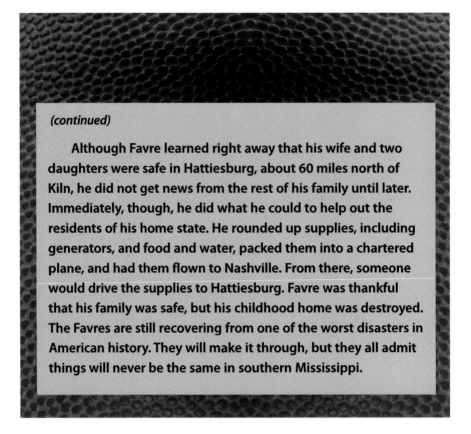

(continued)

Although Favre learned right away that his wife and two daughters were safe in Hattiesburg, about 60 miles north of Kiln, he did not get news from the rest of his family until later. Immediately, though, he did what he could to help out the residents of his home state. He rounded up supplies, including generators, and food and water, packed them into a chartered plane, and had them flown to Nashville. From there, someone would drive the supplies to Hattiesburg. Favre was thankful that his family was safe, but his childhood home was destroyed. The Favres are still recovering from one of the worst disasters in American history. They will make it through, but they all admit things will never be the same in southern Mississippi.

(continued from page 115)

encountered as an NFL player: a shutout. The Chicago Bears, who would go on to play in the Super Bowl that year, soundly defeated the Packers, 26-0. The Packers started the season 1–4 and were again shut out in Week 11, falling to the New England Patriots, 35-0, as Favre was knocked out of the game before halftime. However, there were some positives during the 2006 season. On September 24, Favre became the second quarterback in NFL history (Dan Marino was the first) to throw 400 touchdown passes in his career. He also became the first NFL player to complete 5,000 passes during his career. The Packers won their last four games and finished 8–8; a marked improvement over the 2005 season. Once again, many people wondered if Favre would announce his retirement during the off-season.

Despite the speculation, Favre revealed in February 2007 that he planned to keep playing football for the Packers. He stated that Green Bay had a good nucleus of young players who could enable the Packers to put together a good season in the relatively weak NFC. At this point in his career, Favre knows he is not bulletproof. But he loves the game and wants to continue playing as long as he is able. To that end, Favre continued his remarkable run during the 2007 season by breaking three prominent NFL records. In a 35-13 win over the New York Giants on September 16, he broke John Elway's record for career wins (148). Then, in a 23-16 win against the Minnesota Vikings, on September 30, he eclipsed Dan Marino's record for career touchdown passes (420). Finally, on December 16, Favre broke Marino's passing record of 61,361 yards.

Although he has a bond with the fans of Green Bay, he plans to return to Mississippi after he retires. He bought 460 acres of land in Hattiesburg, an hour from where he grew up. Favre loves Green Bay—the people, the atmosphere, and the football team that courses through his veins. To Favre, though, Hancock County will always be home. "Some people just come from a place," Favre once said. "But I feel like I am that place."

Favre entered the 2007 season believing it would be his last, and he would have gone out with a bang. In 2007, he extended his own NFL record with at least 3,000 passing yards for the 16th consecutive season, surpassing the 4,000 yard mark for the

MOST NFL SEASONS WITH 3,000 OR MORE YARDS PASSING

NUMBER	PLAYER
16	Brett Favre, Green Bay, 1992–2007
13	Dan Marino, Miami, 1984–1992, 1994–1995, 1997–1998
12	John Elway, Denver, 1985–1991, 1993–1997

Many Packers fans speculated whether Brett Favre's last game in a Green Bay uniform would be the team's final game of the 2005 season against the Seattle Seahawks. Fortunately for Green Bay fans, Favre returned for both the 2006 and 2007 seasons.

fifth time in his career. He connected on eight touchdown passes of 40 yards or longer, which was a career high. In addition, he extended his own league mark with three more touchdown passes of 75 yards or more, pushing him up to a career 14. He also tied and broke the league record with his eighth and ninth TD passes of at least 80 yards. For the first time, he threw for at least 300 yards in three consecutive games and accomplished this feat twice in the season. Favre completed 356 of 535 passes for 4,155 yards and 28 TDs, with 15 interceptions, for a 95.7 passer rating. He finished fourth in the league in passing yards, completions and completion percentage. He was named Sports

MOST TOUCHDOWN PASSES IN NFL HISTORY

NUMBER	PLAYER
442	Brett Favre, Atlanta, 1991; Green Bay, 1992–2006
420	Dan Marino, Miami, 1983–1999
342	Fran Tarkenton, Minnesota, 1961–1966, 1972–1978; New York Giants, 1967–1971

Illustrated's "Sportsman of the Year," playing some of his best football during his seventeenth season. Starting all 16 games, he brought his career total to 253 consecutive regular-season starts, second most in NFL history. After Green Bay's loss to the New York Giants in the NFC Championship game, Favre still wouldn't give a sure answer on whether or not he would retire. But Favre had been flirting with retirement the entire season, and Packer fans thought they would have to bid farewell to perhaps their most beloved player. They never could have imagined, though, what kind of a goodbye it would turn out to be.

On March 6, 2008, Favre held a tearful retirement press conference. The decision had been made—Favre was leaving the Pack. During the summer, however, he had second thoughts. He wasn't sure he wanted to retire after all, but he wasn't sure if he wanted to stay in Green Bay, either. Apparently, Favre had been making phone calls to Viking's offensive coordinator Darrell Bevell, who used to be an assistant in Green Bay. These calls sparked a heated controversy in the NFL. The Packers thought Favre's discussions with Bevell had violated league rules. Certainly, the Pack did not want Favre signing on with one of their biggest rivals. As it turned out, Favre wasn't destined for Minnesota. Instead, he signed a deal with the New York Jets, keeping his trademark jersey number. It's probably not surprising Favre picked the Jets. He seems to play well in green.

BRETT FAVRE
POSITION: **Quarterback**

FULL NAME: **Brett Lorenzo Favre**
BORN: **October 10, 1969,
Gulfport, Mississippi**
HEIGHT: **6'2"**
WEIGHT: **222 lbs.**
COLLEGE: **Southern Mississippi**

TEAMS: **Atlanta
Falcons (1991),
Green Bay Packers
(1992–Present)**

YEAR	TEAM	G	COMP	ATT	PCT	YD	Y/A	TD	INT
1991	ATL	2	0	4	0.0	0	0.0	0	2
1992	GNB	15	302	471	64.1	3,227	6.9	18	13
1993	GNB	16	318	522	60.9	3,303	6.3	19	24
1994	GNB	16	363	582	62.4	3,882	6.7	33	14
1995	GNB	16	359	570	63.0	4,413	7.7	38	13
1996	GNB	16	325	543	59.9	3,899	7.2	39	13
1997	GNB	16	304	513	59.3	3,867	7.5	35	16
1998	GNB	16	347	551	63.0	4,212	7.6	31	23
1999	GNB	16	341	595	57.3	4,091	6.9	22	23
2000	GNB	16	338	580	58.3	3,812	6.6	20	16
2001	GNB	16	314	510	61.6	3,921	7.7	32	15
2002	GNB	16	341	551	61.9	3,658	6.6	27	16
2003	GNB	16	308	471	65.4	3,361	7.1	32	21
2004	GNB	16	346	540	64.1	4,088	7.6	30	17
2005	GNB	16	372	607	61.3	3,881	6.4	20	29
2006	GNB	16	343	613	56.0	3,885	6.3	18	18
2007	GNB	16	356	535	66.5	4,155	7.8	28	15
TOTALS		257	5,377	8,758	61.4	61,655	7.0	442	288

CHRONOLOGY

1969   October 10 Brett Lorenzo Favre is born in Gulfport, Mississippi.

1979   In fifth grade, begins playing the position he will play for the rest of his life—quarterback.

1982   Officially begins dating Deanna.

1983–1987   At Hancock North Central High School in Kiln, Mississippi, excels at both baseball and football; in baseball, he leads the team in batting for five seasons, and on the gridiron, he plays strong safety, punter, and place kicker, as well as quarterback.

1987   Accepts a scholarship from the University of Southern Mississippi; on September 19, he plays the second half of the game against Tulane, guiding the Golden Eagles to a 31-24 comeback win.

1989   February Daughter Brittany is born.

1991   Picked by the Atlanta Falcons in the second round—thirty-third overall—of the NFL draft.

1992   Traded to Green Bay in February; in September, against the Cincinnati Bengals, he replaces first-string quarterback Don Majkowski in the fourth quarter and leads a five-play, 92-yard drive, capped by a 35-yard touchdown pass to give the Packers a 24-23 victory.

1993   February At age 23, becomes the youngest quarterback to earn a trip to the NFL Pro Bowl.

1994   January 8 Leads the Packers to a thrilling 28-24 win against the Detroit Lions, giving Green Bay its first playoff victory since 1982.

1994   December Sets a Packers record with 33 touchdown passes and 363 completions in a season, and Green Bay makes the playoffs for the second-straight year.

1995   **February 5** Goes to another Pro Bowl, where he is the NFC's starting quarterback.

Sets a single-season Packers record with 38 touchdown passes and leads the NFL with 4,413 passing yards, earning him the NFL MVP Award.

1996   **January 6** Leads the Packers to wins over the Atlanta Falcons and San Francisco 49ers to advance to the NFC Championship Game for the first time since 1967.

January 14 Packers lose to the Dallas Cowboys in the NFC Championship Game.

March Enters rehab for an addiction to painkillers.

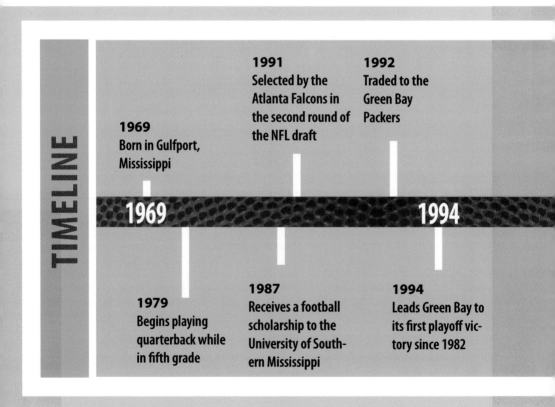

TIMELINE

1969
Born in Gulfport, Mississippi

1991
Selected by the Atlanta Falcons in the second round of the NFL draft

1992
Traded to the Green Bay Packers

1969

1994

1979
Begins playing quarterback while in fifth grade

1987
Receives a football scholarship to the University of Southern Mississippi

1994
Leads Green Bay to its first playoff victory since 1982

July 14 Marries Deanna.

December 30 Breaks his own record with 39 touchdown passes and earns the NFL MVP Award for the second year in a row.

1997   January 26 Packers beat the New England Patriots, 35-21, in Super Bowl XXXI.

December 27 Becomes the first NFL player to win the NFL MVP Award three times in career.

1998   January 25 In Super Bowl XXXII, the Packers lose to the Denver Broncos, 31-24, in San Diego.

December 20 Against the Tennessee Oilers, throws his thirtieth touchdown pass of the season for the fifth

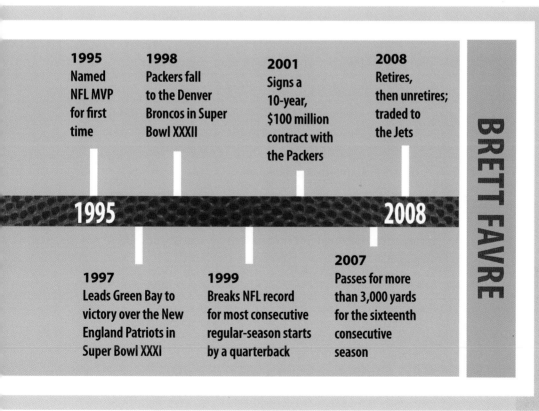

1995 Named NFL MVP for first time

1998 Packers fall to the Denver Broncos in Super Bowl XXXII

2001 Signs a 10-year, $100 million contract with the Packers

2008 Retires, then unretires; traded to the Jets

1995   2008

BRETT FAVRE

1997 Leads Green Bay to victory over the New England Patriots in Super Bowl XXXI

1999 Breaks NFL record for most consecutive regular-season starts by a quarterback

2007 Passes for more than 3,000 yards for the sixteenth consecutive season

year in a row, overtaking Dan Marino's record for most consecutive seasons with 30 or more touchdown passes.

1999   July 13 Second daughter, Breleigh, is born.

November 7 Breaks Ron Jaworski's record for most consecutive regular-season starts by a quarterback with 117.

December 12 In his one hundred twenty-sixth professional game, reaches 30,000-yard plateau for passing yards, becoming the third-fastest quarterback in history to reach this milestone.

2000   December 24 Earns one hundredth win as a professional when the Packers defeat Tampa Bay in overtime, 17-14.

2001   February 28 Signs a 10-year, $100 million contract with the Packers.

2002   January 13 Packers take a 25-15 victory over San Francisco in the NFC wild-card game.

January 20 Quarterbacks the worst game of his career in a 45-17 loss to the Rams in the divisional playoffs; he throws six interceptions in the game—a career high and an NFL postseason record.

2005   After 13 consecutive nonlosing seasons, the Packers finish 4–12; still, Favre throws for more than 3,000 yards for the fourteenth consecutive season, an NFL record.

2006   April Announces he will be playing in the 2006 season; the Packers finish with an 8–8 record.

2007   February Reveals that he will play again for the Packers in the 2007 season.

Breaks John Elway's record for career victories (148); breaks Dan Marino's record of 420 career touchdown passes and passing yards (61,361).

2008   **March 6** Holds press conference on March 6 to announce his retirement. Although Favre later decides to return to the NFL, he is traded to the New York Jets.

September 28 In the fourth game of the 2008-2009 season, Favre throws a career-high six touchdown passes in a 56-35 victory against the Arizona Cardinals, the Jets second most points in a single game in franchise history.

GLOSSARY

American Football Conference (AFC)   One of the two conferences in the National Football League (NFL). The AFC was established after the NFL merged with the American Football League (AFL) in 1970.

audible   A play called by the quarterback at the line of scrimmage to change the play that was called in the huddle.

backfield   The football players whose positions are behind the line of scrimmage; or the area where these players line up.

backup   A second-string player who does not start the game, but comes in later in relief of a starter.

blitz   A defensive maneuver in which one or more linebackers or defensive backs, who normally remain behind the line of scrimmage, instead charge into the opponent's backfield.

blocking   When a player obstructs another player's path with his body. Examples: cut block, zone block, trap block, pull block, screen block, pass block, and double-team block.

bootleg   An offensive play predicated upon misdirection in which the quarterback pretends to hand the ball to another player and then carries the ball in the opposite direction of the supposed ballcarrier with the intent of either passing or running (sometimes the quarterback has the option of doing either).

center   A player position on offense. The center snaps the ball.

chain   The 10-yard-long chain that is used by the chain crew (aka, "chain gang") to measure for a new series of downs.

completion percentage   The percentage of passes thrown by a player that are completed. For example, if a running back throws one pass all season and completes it, his completion percentage would be 100 percent.

cornerback   A defensive back who lines up near the line of scrimmage across from a wide receiver. His primary job is to disrupt passing routes and to defend against short and medium passes in the passing game and to contain the rusher on running plays.

cover two   Zone coverage with the safeties playing deep and covering half the field each.

defensive back   A cornerback or safety position on the defensive team; commonly defends against wide receivers on passing plays. Generally there are four defensive backs playing at a time.

defensive end   A player position on defense who lines up on the outside of the defensive line whose principal function is to deliver pressure to the quarterback.

defensive tackle   A player position on defense on the inside of the defensive line whose principal function is to contain the run.

depth chart   A player's position on the roster; for example, Brett Favre joined the Southern Mississippi football team as a seventh-string quarterback.

drive   A continuous set of offensive plays gaining substantial yardage and several first downs, usually leading to a scoring opportunity.

drop back   When a quarterback takes a few steps back into the pocket after taking the snap to set up for the pass.

end zone   The area between the end line and the goal line, bounded by the sidelines.

extra point   A single point scored in a conversion attempt after a touchdown by place- or drop-kicking the ball through the opponent's goal.

field goal   Score of three points made by place- or drop-kicking the ball through the opponent's goal.

first down   The first of a set of four downs. Usually, a team that has a first down needs to advance the ball 10 yards to receive another first down, but penalties or field position (i.e., less than 10 yards from the opposing end zone) can affect this.

formation   An arrangement of the offensive skill players.

fourth down   The final of a set of four downs. Unless a first down is achieved or a penalty forces a replay of the down, the team will lose control of the ball after this play. If a team does not think they can get a first down, they often punt on fourth down or kick a field goal if they are close enough to do so.

fullback   A player position on offense. In modern formations, this position may be varied, and this player has more blocking responsibilities in comparison to the halfback or tailback.

fumble   A ball that a player accidentally loses possession of.

goal line   The front of the end zone.

guard   One of two player positions on offense (linemen).

handoff   A player's handing of a live ball to another player. The handoff goes either backwards or laterally, as opposed to a forward pass.

holding   There are two kinds of holding: offensive holding, illegally blocking a player from the opposing team by grabbing and holding his uniform or body; and defensive holding, called against defensive players who impede receivers who are more than five yards from the line of scrimmage, but who are not actively making an attempt to catch the ball.

huddle   An on-field gathering of members of a team in order to secretly communicate instructions for the upcoming play.

I formation   A formation that includes a fullback and tailback lined up with the fullback directly in front of the tailback. If a third back is in line, this is referred to as a "full house I" or "Maryland I." If the third back is lined up alongside the fullback, it is referred to as a "Power I."

incomplete pass   A forward pass of the ball that no player legally caught.

interception   The legal catching of a forward pass thrown by an opposing player.

kickoff   A free kick that starts each half, or restarts the game following a touchdown or field goal.

line of scrimmage/scrimmage line   One of two vertical planes parallel to the goal line where the ball is to be put in play by scrimmage.

linebacker   A player position on defense. The linebackers typically play one to six yards behind the defensive linemen and are the most versatile players on the field because they can play both run and pass defense or are called to blitz.

man-to-man coverage   A defense in which all players in pass coverage, typically linebackers and defensive backs, cover a specific player.

move the chains   Using first downs to drive a team, play by play, toward its opponent's end zone.

National Collegiate Athletic Association (NCAA)   Principal governing body of college sports, including college football.

National Football Conference (NFC)   One of the two conferences in the National Football League (NFL). The NFC was established after the NFL merged with the American Football League (AFL) in 1970.

National Football League (NFL)   The largest professional American football league, with 32 teams.

offside   An infraction of the rule that requires both teams to be on their own side of their restraining line as or before the ball is put in play. Offside is typically called on the defensive team.

off-tackle   A running play designed to go to the strong side and take advantage of the hole created by the tackle, tight end, and fullback.

option   A type of play in which the quarterback has the option of handing off, keeping, or laterally passing to one or more backs. Often described by a type of formation or play action, such as triple option, veer option, or counter option.

pass interference   When a player illegally hinders an eligible receiver's opportunity to catch a forward pass.

passer rating (*also* **quarterback rating**)   A numeric value used to measure the performance of quarterbacks. It was formulated in 1973 and it uses the player's completion percentage, passing yards, touchdowns, and interceptions.

play action   A tactic in which the quarterback fakes either a handoff or a throw in order to draw the defense away from the intended offensive method.

pocket   An area on the offensive side of the line of scrimmage, where the offensive linemen attempt to prevent the defensive players from reaching the quarterback during passing plays.

position   A place where a player plays relative to teammates, and/or a role filled by that player.

punt   A kick in which the ball is dropped and kicked before it reaches the ground. Used to give up the ball to the opposition after offensive downs have been used.

quarterback   An offensive player who lines up behind the center, from whom he takes the snap.

reception   When a player catches (receives) the ball.

redshirt   In college, when a football player sits out for one year but does not lose a year of eligibility; college players only have four years in which they are eligible to play.

running back   A player position on offense. Although the term usually refers to the halfback or tailback, fullbacks are also considered running backs.

sack   Tackling a ballcarrier who intends to throw a forward pass. A sack is also awarded if a player forces a fumble of the ball or the ballcarrier to go out of bounds, behind the line of scrimmage on an apparent intended forward pass play.

safety   A player position on defense; a method of scoring (worth two points) by downing an opposing ballcarrier in his own end zone, forcing the opposing ballcarrier out of his own end zone and out of bounds, or forcing the offensive team to fumble the ball so that it exits the end zone.

scramble   On a called passing play, when the quarterback runs from the pocket in an attempt to avoid being sacked, giving the receivers more time to get open or attempting to gain positive yards by running himself.

secondary   Refers to the defensive "backfield," specifically the safeties and cornerbacks.

shotgun formation   Formation in which offensive team may line up at the start of a play. In this formation, the quarterback receives the snap five to eight yards behind the center.

sideline   One of the lines marking each side of the field.

snap   The handoff or pass from the center that begins a play from scrimmage.

special teams   The units that handle kickoffs, punts, free kicks, and field-goal attempts.

starter   A player who is the first to play his position within a given game or season. Depending on the position and the game situation, this player may be replaced or share time with one or more players later in the game. For example, a quarterback may start the game but be replaced by a backup quarterback if the game becomes one-sided.

T formation   A classic offensive formation with the quarterback directly behind the center and three running backs behind the quarterback, forming a "T." Numerous variations have been developed, including the Split-T, Wing-T, and Wishbone-T.

tackle   The act of forcing a ballcarrier to the ground. Also, a position on the offensive and defensive line.

tailback   Player position on offense farthest ("deepest") back, except in kicking formations.

tight end   A player position on offense, often known as a Y receiver when he lines up on the line of scrimmage, next to the offensive tackle. Tight ends are used as blockers during running plays and either run a route or stay in to block during passing plays.

time of possession   The amount of time one team has the ball in its possession relative to the other team.

toss sweep   A running play in which the quarterback tosses the ball to the tailback who follows a pulling guard toward the outside or cuts back if there is room to run.

touchdown   A play worth six points, accomplished by gaining legal possession of the ball in the opponent's end zone. It also allows the team a chance for one extra point by kicking the ball or a chance to attempt a two-point conversion.

turnover   The loss of the ball by one team to the other team. This is usually the result of a fumble or an interception.

West Coast offense   An offensive philosophy that uses short, high-percentage passes as the core of a ball-control offense.

wide receiver   A player position on offense. He is split wide (usually about 10 yards) from the formation and plays on the line of scrimmage as a split end (X) or one yard off as a flanker (Z).

wild card   The two playoff spots given to the two nondivision winning teams that have the best records in each conference.

wishbone   A formation involving three running backs lined up behind the quarterback in the shape of a Y, similar to the shape of a wishbone.

yard   One yard of linear distance in the direction of one of the two goals. A field is 100 yards. Typically, a team is required to advance at least 10 yards in order to get a new set of downs.

zone defense   A defense in which players who are in pass coverage cover zones of the field, instead of individual players.

BIBLIOGRAPHY

"Favre, McNair Lead Katrina Relief Efforts." *Chicago Sun Times*, September 1, 2005. Available online at *http://findarticles.com/p/articles/mi_qn4155/is_20050901/ai_n15651324*.

Braun, Rick. "Packers Notebook: Favre Frets for Family in Path of Katrina." *Milwaukee Journal Sentinel*, September 1, 2005. Available online at *http://findarticles.com/p/articles/mi_qn4196/is_20050901/ai_n15337226*.

D'Amato, Gary. "Packers Feel the Effects of Katrina." *Milwaukee Journal Sentinel*, September 1, 2005. Available online at *http://findarticles.com/p/articles/mi_qn4196/is_20060205/ai_n16051433*.

Favre, Brett. *Favre: For the Record*. New York: Doubleday, 1997.

———, and Bonita Favre. *Favre*. New York: Rugged Land, 2004.

———, and Marc Serota. *Favre: Most Valuable Player*. Hallendale, Fla.: EGI Productions, 1999.

Goska, Eric. *Green Bay Packers: A Measure of Greatness*. Iola, Wisc.: Krause Publications, 2003.

Havel, Chris. "Bonita Favre Tells Her Harrowing Katrina Tale." USATODAY.com. Available online at *http://www.usatoday.com/sports/football/nfl/packers/2005-09-15-bonita-katrina_x.htm*.

King, Peter. "Warmed Up." *Sports Illustrated*, January 27, 1997, 70–74.

Milwaukee Journal Sentinel. Available online at *http://www.jsonline.com*.

The Official Web site of the National Football League. Available online at *http://www.nfl.com*.

Nickel, Lori. "Brett Favre Reflects on Hurricane Katrina." *Milwaukee Journal Sentinel*, September 1, 2006. Available online at *http://findarticles.com/p/articles/mi_qn4196/is_20060901/ai_n16711977*.

The Official Web site of the Green Bay Packers. Available
   online at *http://www.Packers.com.*

Pro-Football-Reference.com. Available online at *http://www.
   profootballreference.com.*

Silver, Michael. "All Packed." *Sports Illustrated*, December 23,
   2002, 38–41.

Sports Illustrated. Available online at *http://www.si.com.*

Starr, Bart, Bonita Favre, Irv Favre, Ray Nischke, et al. *Brett
   Favre Uncovered: By the People Who Know Him Best.* Dallas,
   Tex.: Beckett Publications, 1997.

The Official Web site of the Super Bowl. "Super Bowl XXXII,
   Denver 31, Green Bay 24." SuperBowl.com. Available online
   at *http://www.superbowl.com/history/recaps/game/sbxxxii.*

FURTHER READING

Favre, Brett. *Favre: For the Record*. New York: Doubleday, 1997.

———, and Bonita Favre. *Favre*. New York: Rugged Land, 2004.

Gulbrandsen, Don. *Green Bay Packers: The Complete Illustrated History*. Osceola, Wisc.: Voyageur Press, 2007.

Gutman, Bill. *Brett Favre: A Biography*. New York: Simon Spotlight Entertainment, 1998.

Nelson, Sharlene, and Ted Nelson. *Brett Favre*. Mankato, Minn.: Capstone Press, 2006.

Povletich, William. *Green Bay Packers: Legends in Green and Gold*. Chicago: Arcadia Publishing, 2005.

WEB SITES

Brett Favre of the Green Bay Packers
www.brettfavre.com

Packers Plus Online
www.jsonline.com/index/index.aspx?id=44

Official Site of the National Football League
www.NFL.com

The Official Web site of Brett Favre
www.officialbrettfavre.com

Official Web site of the Green Bay Packers
www.packers.com

PICTURE CREDITS

INDEX

ABOUT THE AUTHOR

RACHEL A. KOESTLER-GRACK has worked with nonfiction books as an editor and writer since 1999. During her career, she has worked extensively with historical topics, ranging from the Middle Ages to the colonial era to the civil rights movement. In addition, she has written numerous biographies on a variety of historical and contemporary figures. Rachel lives with her husband and daughter on a hobby farm near Glencoe, Minnesota.